Grammar School Appeals

Contents

Appeals' Procedures

Appeals' Procedures

Appeals can be worth pursuing if your child has missed the pass mark by a few points. However, most appeals are not successful due to the pressure on places in the grammar schools. It is not always clear why some succeed and others do not. It can depend on the make up of the committee, the school you are applying for and the presentation of the appeal on the day. For the best chance of success it is essential that the accompanying statement that goes with your appeal form, the **'Grounds for Appeal'** is properly prepared. Our experience shows that when appeals are prepared and presented following the examples in this book, the chance of success is greatly improved.

1. Applying for an Appeal's Form to fill in and returning it as the basis for appeal. This form is often supplied with your results letter and will need to be returned by the date stated. Late appeals will not be considered.

2. The most important part of this form is the **'Grounds for Appeal'**. This should be typed and carefully worded. This booklet gives examples of past appeal statements for your reference. Look through and adapt one or more of them and this will help you write your appeal in the same objective style. This is crucial to your success as emotionally charged appeals do not generally succeed. Do ensure your spelling and grammar are thoroughly checked before submission.

3. The **Focus** of the **'Grounds for Appeal'** should concentrate on one main point and everything in the statement should drive this point home. It is not advisable to focus on more than one main issue as this can 'muddy' the appeal and weaken its impact.

4. The **'Grounds for Appeal'** normally centre around one of **three issues**:

a. Academic - My child should have passed this examination on academic grounds and there is strong evidence to support the fact they should have passed (copies of school reports can be included, predicted SATs scores for next year if you know them, teachers reports and any independent verification possible). A supportive head teacher who will write a letter to verify your child's ability will he helpful. References about tuition are normally damaging as it may lead the panel to think the child should have passed anyway if he or she received help. AE Tuition does not generally provide letters of support for this very reason, as it can prejudice your position with the appeal panel. If your child has dyslexia, dyspraxia, Attention Deficit Hyperactive Disorder (ADHD) or some other recognised disability that may have affected their result, evidence can be submitted to show that it may have caused them to under achieve in the examination. Some good examples are given of past appeal letters that deal with children who have special needs.

4

b. Health - Your child was ill on the day and in hindsight should not have sat the examination; or became ill during the examination. If you have verification this will help i.e. a doctor's certificate that was sought either prior or post the exam. If there is an ongoing medical problem, that may have affected their performance, medical evidence can also be submitted to show that they may have under performed for this reason and this can be taken into account in the final decision. Medical records from consultants are very useful; particularly if they are current.

c. Circumstantial - If there are difficulties at home i.e. the break-up of a marriage or partnership, the serious illness or death of a close relative or some other serious trauma, this can be 'Grounds for Appeal'. A child's performance can be seriously affected by such circumstances. Documentary evidence, dates of particularly traumatic incidents and any record or evidence detailing the child's reaction can be submitted for consideration at appeal.

5. The **'Grounds for Appeal'** should generally be no longer than one side A4 unless there are special reasons that require further clarification. Long and wordy appeals tend to be diffuse and less effective.

6. If the child on appeal has a **Sibling** in the school already, or is the sibling of another child who has passed in the same year e.g. a twin (or cousin), the emotional bond can be offered as a subsidiary reason for the appeal. This may also be supported by the awkwardness of travel arrangements for separate children etc. However this should not usually be a main 'Grounds for Appeal', unless it can be argued that separating the children will have a very damaging effect for both of them. Be aware that, as competition for places becomes tighter, 'Grounds for Appeal' on this basis have been received less favourably.

7. On occasions **'unusual circumstances'** can affect the performance of a child in the examination and this can be 'Grounds for Appeal'. e.g. the exam was not conducted in a proper manner; or a child was continually distracted by another child in the exam room or something distressing or traumatic happened on the day of the exam etc.

8. The **head teacher's support** is essential and it is advisable to book an appointment to discuss the appeal. They may have to write a report on your child and it is important they are positive and do not make negative comments. Make it clear you have decided to go to appeal and you want his or her support. Do not have a meeting to decide whether you will appeal. Tell your head teacher that you will appeal and it is essential that they support you otherwise your chances of winning it will be severely damaged. Ask to see any letter of support they may write if possible and make another appointment with them if you do not consider it to be supportive. Some head teachers will not allow you to see what they write, but it is worth asking for a copy. If possible, you want the letter to say that it is likely your child will achieve **two level 5s in their SATs tests** the following May. This kind of verification will be looked upon very favourably by an appeal panel as they would have expected a child with high SATs scores to pass the 11+.

9. The **Appeal Hearing - Always elect to be present.** It is never a good idea to allow an appeal to be decided without you being present as your attendance will give emotional weight to the appeal. This will involve **Meeting the Appeals Committee** made up of at least one educational representative (possibly from the school of choice). A representative from the local authority or exam setting body will be present initially to present the case. They will leave once this has been completed so the appeal committee can discuss the issues and come to a decision. It is important that you stress the same points you made in your original **'Grounds for Appeal'**. Read through your **'Grounds for Appeal'** and take notes so you can reiterate them in the hearing. Do not be side-tracked, but simply give more detail to substantiate your appeal. Wavering from your original argument will make it look as if your appeal was based on weak grounds to begin with. Be positive and direct as in your 'Grounds for Appeal'. Do not be tempted to introduce new information as they will wonder why this was not included originally (unless further evidence that can be substantiated has come to light since you submitted your appeal). If your command of the English language is weak or you do not feel confident in putting forth a clear and concise argument based on your **'Grounds for Appeal'** take someone with you who has these skills to speak on your behalf. Often another relative or friend, who you trust can articulate your argument clearly and assist you in the appeal.

11. The **Appeals' Committee will write** to you to communicate their decision. If an appeal is unsuccessful it can be referred to an **Ombudsman** if you think there are grounds to suggest the appeal was **not fairly heard**. This can occur if significant evidence was overlooked or the appeal was conducted in such a way as to not give you a fair opportunity to make your case clearly and effectively. The ombudsman will not examine the content of the appeal, but only whether the procedure was 'fair' and your case was properly considered.

    Legal representation can be sought if you believe an appeal panel has not judged a case fairly. This must be done within three months of the case being heard. Obviously a letter from a solicitor with experience in the educational field would be the first stage. Unless you are sure of your grounds it could be very expensive to proceed beyond this stage.

    Your **M.P.** can also be contacted if you consider you have been treated in an unjust or prejudicial way. In the first instance, a meeting with your M.P. can be arranged at the M.P.'s surgery. At this meeting it is useful to provide a copy of all the documentation with a covering letter summarising the main contents and the basis of your complaint.

Structuring your 'Grounds for Appeal'

Structuring your 'Grounds for Appeal' Statement

The following plan is a useful guide:

1. **Heading - name of child** and **date of birth**.

2. The **school** you are appealing for and the **score achieved**.

3. The **child's achievements** in English, Maths and Science and predicted SATs scores. Include anything that validates ability level and why he/she should have achieved the desired score. If the head teacher supports you, then this should be stated and a supporting letter provided.

4. **Reasons for** and **evidential support if necessary to** show why your child did not achieve the desired score. It is best to focus on one main area:
    a. **Academic** (should have achieved it, but under achieved on the day - this may have some circumstantial or health reasons linked to it).
    b. **Health** (your child was sick on the day or prior to the exam and this may have affected performance).
    c. **Circumstantial** (some tragic family event or emotional trauma that deeply affected your child's performance).
    Note - Do not be tempted to argue on all three grounds as this will weaken your appeal. One main reason and supporting assertions is the best approach to take. Official letters from doctors and any form of written proof that validates your reasons should be included as evidence.

5. **A Concluding statement** affirming that you believe your child is deserving of a grammar school place. You can reiterate your main reason for this, to ensure that the appeal committee has understood why your child should have succeeded in the examination.

Examples of Appeals

Academic Reasons

Example 1 - Academic

Appeal for *(Child's name)* (Date of birth dd/mm/yy)

We wish to appeal for direct entry to *(name of school)* on the grounds that *(Child's name)* passed the 11+ examination with the required score of 111.

(Child's name) is a highly motivated, intelligent and academically capable child who is deserving of a grammar school placement. As she has achieved a pass score we also believe that she has demonstrated very clearly that she is well suited to a grammar school education.

(Child's name) has performed extremely well in all areas of the curriculum throughout the years of her primary education. She is predicted to achieve level 5 or 5* in the three core subjects of Mathematics, English and Science in her Key Stage 2 SATs in May this year. *(Child's name)* did very well on the NFER practice papers (scoring in excess of 85%) in Verbal Reasoning, Non-verbal Reasoning, Mathematics and this influenced our decision to let her sit for the 11+ examination. *(Child's name)* is a high achiever and given the opportunity to attend *(name of school)* will no doubt fulfil her true potential.

We understand there is an emphasis on the importance of Science and technology skills at *(name of school)*. *(Child's name)* has demonstrated she has excellent ICT skills in her primary school and loves using the computer at home too. She regularly logs onto the internet to gather information and to contact family and friends in different parts of the world. *(Child's name)* is also very adept at using the computer for homework assignments and research purposes. She has a thirst for knowledge and has a special interest in science. In particular she is fascinated with astronomy and the current space programmes. It is hard to keep *(Child's name)* supplied with interesting material as she absorbs information so quickly. We believe that *(name of school)* will support and advance *(Child's name)*'s special interest in the areas of science and technology to the very highest level.

There are excellent facilities at *(name of school)* for sport and *(Child's name)* would thrive in this environment. She loves all sports but is particularly keen on basketball and football and we know the school will be able to encourage and support this interest. *(Child's name)* is already a model student of a martial art. After starting only 15 months ago she has passed 3 grading sessions, won 2 silver medals and a bronze medal. She loves teamwork and is excited about the prospect of playing competitive games. We believe *(Child's name)*'s potential peer group at *(name of school)* will be highly motivated and competitive like her. This will stimulate *(Child's name)* to aim for the best she can be.

(Child's name) will be a valuable member of the *(name of school)* community. She is a confident well adjusted child who works well on her own and with others. *(Child's name)* is well liked and popular with both her peers and with teachers. She is self-disciplined, always compliant, loves a challenge and wants to succeed in everything she does.

(Name of school) is conveniently located for us. It will enable *(Child's name)* to easily and regularly take part in extra-curricular activities outside school hours; which she is always keen to do. It will also enable us as parents to support *(Child's name)* and the school by attending meetings, going to school functions and helping out at fund raising events.

Example 2 - Academic

Appeal for *(Child's name)* **(Date of birth dd/mm/yy)**

We wish to appeal against the decision not to offer *(Child's name)* a place at *(name of school)* on the grounds that she did not reach the 117 threshold for entry (score of 115).

(Child's name) is a very bright and talented girl. She is highly motivated and conscientious in everything she does. *(Child's name)* has performed exceptionally well in her primary school, impressing her teachers with a high level of dedication and phenomenal work rate. Her school have predicted she will achieve high level 5s in her SATs in all three core subjects with no difficulty at all this year. Both we and her school expected *(Child's name)* to achieve a much higher score in the 11+ examination than she did and that is why we put *(name of school)* as first choice. *(Child's name)*'s head teacher has had no hesitation in supporting this appeal as he believes *(name of school)* will be an ideal place for *(Child's name)* to continue her education.

Although we are very pleased *(Child's name)* achieved a pass score, we are disappointed because she does not have a place at *(name of school)*. We believe that *(Child's name)* underachieved on the day, although it is hard to say why. All the indicators showed she would achieve a very high pass. *(Child's name)* did NFER practice tests in the run up to the examination and scored over 90% on every single paper. We can only conclude that nerves and the sense of occasion might have caused her to under perform.

We believe there are circumstances relevant to the appeal that should he taken into account, although they are somewhat unusual. We know if a child has a sibling in the school that this will be taken into account in any appeal. We are in a difficult situation, as this is not the case. However, *(Child's name)* does have a very close friendship with two other children who have passed and will be going to *(name of school)*. She has been with these two friends since the beginning of her education and they are almost like a sister and a brother to her. The friendships have been of tremendous help to all three children. They support and encourage each other and work together whenever they can. Our family has close ties with the other two families as well and everybody involved is distressed about the possible separation of the children. Most of all, *(Child's name)* is very upset and concerned about losing these relationships. Her confidence has been dented and she feels very insecure at present. *(Child's name)* believed she worked just as hard as the other two children and does not understand why she did not do as well. We believe it will be emotionally damaging for *(Child's name)* to sever this relationship.

Example 3 - Academic

Appeal for *(Child's name)* (Date of birth dd/mm/yy)

We wish to appeal against the decision not to offer *(Child's name)* a place at *(name of school)* on the grounds that he did not reach the 117 threshold for entry (scored 114).

(Child's name) is a very intelligent and well motivated child. He has done exceedingly well in his primary school and is in the top sets for every subject. His school believe that he will achieve high level 5s in all three core subjects in his SATs this year. While preparing for the 11+ he scored over 90% in every NFER practice test in Verbal Reasoning, Mathematics and Non-verbal Reasoning. *(Child's name)*'s head teacher had no hesitation in fully supporting this appeal as he believes *(Child's name)* to be a very bright and gifted child.

All the indicators suggested that *(Child's name)* should have scored higher in the 11+ examination than he did, and that is why we had no hesitation in putting *(name of school)* as our first choice. We believe that *(Child's name)* underachieved on the day of the examination; his score not being representative of his performance generally. We have no specific explanation for this. We do know *(Child's name)* gets very nervous when he is pressurised and this may have caused him to under perform.

We were very pleased that *(Child's name)* achieved a pass score, but disappointed that it would not gain him entry into *(name of school)*. *(Child's name)* had set his heart on this school for very specific reasons.
(Child's name)'s cousin, ***** has secured a place at *(name of school)* and they both planned to start there together. They were very much looking forward to studying and spending time together in their new school. *(Child's name)* and ***** are more like brothers than cousins, and are the very best of friends too. They are never apart in their primary school and spend most of their spare time together as well. *(Child's name)* and ***** are very upset about the prospect of separation after they have spent most of their life together. They greatly value the support and encouragement they receive from each other on a daily basis. As they have never been separated, both families are concerned about the prospect of splitting them up and believe it will damage them psychologically.

As a family we are in the final stages of moving both our home and business to *(name of town)*; completion is expected at the end of this month. We believe that it will be beneficial for *(Child's name)* to be in a grammar school he can walk to. This will allow him to take part in extra-curricular activities and us to fully support the school as parents.

Example 4 - Academic

Appeal for *(Child's name)* **(Date of birth dd/mm/yy)**

We wish to appeal against the decision not to offer *(Child's name)* a place at *(name of school)* on the grounds that he did not achieve the required score of 117 (score of 116).

(Child's name) is a bright, intelligent, talented and well rounded child. He has attained excellent results across all subjects of the curriculum in his primary school. *(Child's name)* is already functioning at level 5 in Maths and Science and we are confident he will achieve level 5 in English by the time he takes his SATs in May *(year)*. This is indicated by his recent success in a national writing competition where he received the runner up prize. The teacher's report enclosed also shows that *(Child's name)* has an excellent aptitude for science. Recently, *(Child's name)* proudly represented the whole of London in the national *(name)* competition and won various medals.

When we selected *(name of school)* as our first choice we were confident that *(Child's name)* would achieve the score. We were of course pleased that *(Child's name)* passed the 11+ examination, but disappointed that he missed the score required for *(name of school)* by just one mark. We do not believe the score he achieved accurately reflects *(Child's name)*'s true ability. We are certain he under achieved on the day due to the very high level of expectation placed upon him and the pressure to perform.

(Child's name) knew there was very intense competition for limited places and made it clear to us on the way to the examination that he felt under intense pressure. At that moment he seemed to have a crisis of confidence and said, "I'll never beat everyone, especially as this is only a fraction of people on one of the testing days." I tried to reassure him, but with no avail and he left us for the examination room upset and emotionally distraught. *(Child's name)* is perhaps a little less mature than some of his peers, as he is one of the youngest children in the year group. He has under-performed before in various activities, when he knows just one mistake can put him out of the running. We believe the intense pressure led him to do just that - under-perform and miss the score by just one mark.

If offered a place, *(Child's name)* would thrive at *(name of school)*. He is enthusiastic, dedicated and determined to reach his true potential.

Example 5 - Academic

Appeal fo*r (Child's name)* (Date of birth dd/mm/yy)

We wish to appeal against the decision not to offer *(Child's name)* a grammar school place on the basis that he did not achieve the required score of 111 (score of 105).

(Child's name) is a bright, academically able and industrious child. He achieved excellent results in all subjects across the curriculum in year 5. His school are confident that he can achieve Level 5 in all three core subjects in his SATs in May *(year)*.

In the run-up to the 11+ examination *(Child's name)* was consistently scoring in excess of 85% in NFER practice papers. In the actual examination he achieved a pass score in Mathematics (115) and Verbal Reasoning (111) as we expected him to. However, for some reason he fell down badly on the Non-verbal Reasoning paper (88). This was very surprising, as in practice tests *(Child's name)* always achieved his best scores in this subject. We have enclosed samples of NFER multiple choice answer sheets as evidence of his consistently high attainment in Non-verbal Reasoning tests.

It is hard to explain why *(Child's name)* failed to achieve the required score in the Non-verbal Reasoning test, when all the indicators suggested this should have been his best score. However, it was the very first test he sat on the day and he said later that he was very nervous. We have noticed that *(Child's name)*, on occasion does have the tendency to rush at things when he is feeling very stressed. As parents, we are aware that he does not adjust easily to new and strange environments, where there are lots of people he does not know. We think he was just overwhelmed by the situation at first, but when he had finally settled down, began to concentrate and focus on what he had to do. This would explain the wide variance in his scoring; a disastrous score on the initial paper and very good scores on the latter two papers.

We are very disappointed that *(Child's name)* did not achieve the required score as we know that he should have passed this examination. *(Child's name)* feels the same way and believes he is well deserving of a grammar school place. The head teacher of his primary school is fully supportive of this appeal, since he expected *(Child's name)* to pass comfortably.

We look forward to hearing from you on the progress of our appeal.

Example 6 - Academic

Appeal for *(Child's name)* (Date of birth dd/mm/yy)

We wish to appeal against the decision not to offer *(Child's name)* a place at *(name of school)* on the grounds that she did not achieve the required score of 117 (score of 115).

(Child's name) is academically bright, self motivated and has consistently achieved excellence over the first five years of her primary schooling. This year she was selected from among many to attend the 'gifted and talented master classes' awarded to children with exceptionally high SATs scores in year 5. This year she is predicted to attain the very highest level in her SATs in May. We are expecting level 5s or 5*s in all three core subjects. As she is the youngest child in her class, this is a remarkable achievement.

(Child's name) has excelled in every area of the curriculum. Recent testing has shown she already has a reading age of 14 years 10 months and a spelling age of 15 years 10 months. *(Child's name)* has also demonstrated she is musically, theatrically and artistically gifted. She is regularly given a significant role to play in these activities within her school.

Naturally we were very pleased that *(Child's name)* achieved a pass score and the prospect of a grammar school place. However we believe *(Child's name)* should have scored well in excess of the required score of 117. In NFER practice tests, *(Child's name)* without difficulty, was scoring consistently over 130 on Verbal Reasoning, Non-verbal Reasoning and Mathematics. We can only assume that on the day, she felt very nervous and overwhelmed by the sense of occasion and did not achieve her usual scores. Therefore we do not regard her performance in the examination as typical or reflective of her true ability level.

(Child's name)'s brother already attends *(name of school)*. He is now in year 11 and performing exceptionally well. She looks up to him and sees him as an example. They have a very close relationship and we believe he will be her mentor, easing her transition from junior to secondary school. As we live in the vicinity of the school, *(Child's name)* will be able to walk to school with her brother. This will be very reassuring for her.

(Child's name) is diligent, enthusiastic and displays a level of maturity rarely found in someone so young. She is very ambitious and determined to reach her full potential. We believe *(name of school)* will best facilitate this.

Example 7 - Academic

Appeal for *(Child's name)* (Date of birth dd/mm/yy)

We wish to appeal against the decision not to offer *(Child's name)* a place at *(name of school)* on the grounds that she did not reach the 111 threshold for entry (*(Child's name)* scored 108).

(Child's name) is an intelligent, very motivated and academically able child. She has done particularly well in her preparatory school over the last year and has shown she is of above average ability. The head teacher of *(name of school)* had no hesitation in fully supporting our appeal and immediately wrote a letter so that we could include it.

In October she achieved an NFER score or 126 (96%) for Mathematics and 110 (74%) for English. Her English score was very good, but the Mathematics score was exceptional. Her school have confirmed that *(Child's name)* is already functioning at level 5 in Mathematics and we are still five months away from the SATs tests this year. We are of course expecting *(Child's name)* to attain straight level 5s in all three core subjects of English, Mathematics and Science at Key Stage 2 SATs. In preparation for the 11+ examination *(Child's name)* did the NFER practice papers and consistently scored over 85% in Verbal Reasoning, Non-verbal Reasoning and Mathematics.

We believe that *(Child's name)* should have passed the 11+ examination as all the indicators suggest, but underachieved on the day. Sometimes *(Child's name)* does lack confidence and this can be reflected in the failure to perform on occasions. Close examination of her reports suggest that she has taken some time to recover from the huge changes that have taken place in the life in the last two years. *(Child's name)* spent much of her younger years in *(country)* until it became too dangerous for us to remain after the September 11th bombing. *(country)* had become *(Child's name)*'s home and she very much liked the British Independent preparatory school in *(country)* she attended. She was doing exceptionally well in this school and seemed to thrive academically. It was very difficult for her to accept returning to the United Kingdom and for some time *(Child's name)*'s performance in school seemed to be affected. *(Child's name)* had to adjust to another way of life in a strange country, in a new home and in a very different type of school. As the youngest child in her year group *(Child's name)* has found it more difficult to make these transitions and we believe her progress was affected.

We believe *(Child's name)* deserves a grammar school placement and has, despite the circumstances performed to a very high level.

Example 8 - Academic

Appeal for *(Child's name)* (Date of birth dd/mm/yy)

We wish to appeal against the decision not to offer *(Child's name)* a grammar school placement on the basis that he did not achieve the required score of 111 (*(Child's name)* scored 109). We appeal on the following academic grounds:

We believe *(Child's name)* should have passed this examination. He is a very bright, well motivated and academically capable child. *(Child's name)* is a high achiever and excels in every subject area across the curriculum. He has attained excellence right through his years of primary schooling and in his new school was placed in the top groups for all subjects, within a very short period. Even in the limited time the school have known him, they have recognised his potential and predicted he will achieve high level 5s or 5*s in all three core subjects of English, Mathematics and Science in his SATs in May this year.

We have received strong support for this appeal from the head teacher of *(name of school)*, who believes that *(Child's name)* will do very well in a grammar school. In fact, it is at the school's original suggestion that we entered *(Child's name)* for the 11+ examination in the first place. *(Child's name)* joined the school on the *** September **** and his class teacher quickly ascertained he was very bright. When we met with him some weeks later for a consultation, he suggested *(Child's name)* should sit the examination.

By now it was mid-October and we knew nothing about the format of the 11+ examination or what kind of preparation might be required for *(Child's name)* to achieve a good result. We set about obtaining some NFER practice papers that had been recommended to us and *(Child's name)* completed them all. His scores improved very quickly in all three subjects: Mathematics, Verbal Reasoning and Non-verbal Reasoning; on the last three papers he scored over 85% in each subject area. *(Child's name)* did feel confident that he had passed and was obviously very disappointed, as we all were when the results came through.

(Child's name) has needed to adjust to many changes in the last few months and it has been very stressful for him - a new home - a new school - the loss of all his friends and a new peer group to negotiate; and then he was suddenly faced with an important examination, with little or no time to prepare for it. It is no wonder he under achieved, as he was feeling very insecure and under so much pressure. We have no doubt that under 'normal circumstances' *(Child's name)* would have passed this examination without difficulty.

Example 9 - Academic

Appeal for *(Child's name)* (Date of birth dd/mm/yy)

We wish to appeal against the decision not to offer *(Child's name)* a place at *(name of school)* on the basis that she did not achieve the required score of 111 (score of 107).

We believe *(Child's name)* should have passed this examination. She is a bright, well-motivated and academically capable child. She has done very well in her Primary School and is in the top groups for English and Mathematics. Her teacher is confident she will achieve excellent results when she takes her SATs in May.

Her end of Year 5 report for Mathematics states:-
"*(Child's name)* has worked hard this year with excellent results. She has gained confidence and is able to apply her existing knowledge to problem solving"

For English they wrote:-
"*(Child's name)* has worked very hard to meet the challenge of the high ability group and has made good progress. She has an excellent vocabulary, which she uses to great effect in her written work. She reads a wide range of texts with expression".

We expect her to score three SATs level 5s in English, Mathematics and Science.

In the run up to the 11+ examination, *(Child's name)* was scoring 80%-85% in the NFER practice tests. In the actual examination she achieved a pass score in Verbal Reasoning (115). However, for some reason she fell down on the Mathematics (99) and the Non-verbal Reasoning paper (106). We have enclosed samples of NFER multiple choice answer sheets as evidence of her usual standard.

It is hard to explain why *(Child's name)* failed to achieve the required score in the Mathematics and Non-Verbal Reasoning tests. We can only conclude that nerves and the sense of occasion might have caused her to under perform. Therefore we do not regard her performance in the examinations as typical of her true ability level.

(Child's name)'s brother already attends *(name of school)*. He is now in year 8 and is making good progress. They have a close relationship and we hope he will help to ease her transition from junior to secondary school. As we live some distance from the school, *(Child's name)* would be able to make the bus journey with her brother. This will be very reassuring for her and for us.

If offered a place we believe *(Child's name)* would thrive at *(name of school)*. She would be a valuable member of the school community. She is a mature well-adjusted child who works well on her own and with others. She enjoys a variety of activities. Currently she is learning to play the oboe and is a member of various sports clubs outside of school.

We look forward to hearing from you on the progress of our appeal.

Example 10 - Academic

Appeal for *(Child's name)* (Date of birth dd/mm/yy)

On behalf of our daughter *(Child's name)* we would like to appeal against the decision not to offer her a place at *(name of school)* on the grounds that she did not reach the 111 threshold for entry, (*(Child's name)* scored 108).

(Child's name) is a bright, conscientious student, who passed the maths and verbal reasoning papers, (112 and 111 respectively), but was let down by the non-verbal reasoning paper (101). Prior to the test, *(Child's name)* demonstrated she had confidence and aptitude in doing non-verbal reasoning papers. It is hard for us to explain why *(Child's name)* missed the 111 score in non-verbal reasoning, when all the pre-test indicators suggested this should have been the area she excelled in. *(Child's name)* came out of the test upset, knowing that she had under-performed in her strongest paper.

(Child's name) is an exceptional student, who is hard working and self motivated. Her head teacher and form teachers for both years 5 and 6 were shocked to learn that she missed a pass by 3 marks, when a 'pass with flying colours' was expected. So much so they had no hesitation in supporting our appeal, (enclosures 1, 2 and 3, letters of recommendation from Headteacher, current form teacher and year 5 form teacher respectively). Throughout *(Child's name)*'s primary school years she has consistently performed above average for her age and at the end of year 5 was already achieving levels 4 and 5 in English, Mathematics and Science, (see enclosure 4, end of year report). Her performance has continued to improve in year 6, and *(Child's name)* is predicted to achieve high level 5's across all subjects in the forthcoming SATs tests in May, (enclosure 2 - recommendation from form teacher).

In addition to *(Child's name)*'s academic achievements, she is also talented at sports and has represented her school in many areas, from individual performance events like swimming, cross-country and athletics to team events like handball and netball. Outside school *(Child's name)* is interested in tennis, which she has been playing since she was 5 years old, and is currently a member of *(name)* Tennis Club, (enclosure 5 - letter from *(Child's name)*'s Tennis Coach). She also has an interest in the Arts and attends dance school where she learns both Jazz and Ballet (enclosure 6 - letter from *(Child's name)*'s dance school teacher).

We believe a medical circumstance may have had some bearing on *(Child's name)*'s performance. Her final week of preparation was punctuated by the need for emergency dental treatment two days before the test, (see enclosure 7 - dentist's report). *(Child's name)* experienced severe pain from an upper molar, which seriously disturbed her sleep for two consecutive nights and prevented her from completing her NFER practice tests for these final two evenings. This was important pre-test preparation.

(Child's name) has an older sister *(name)*, currently in year 8, and a cousin, currently

in year 7, who she is close to and would receive support from in the transition to secondary school. We believe *(Child's name)* would thrive at *(name of school)*. She would also put a lot back into *(name of school)* in terms of her extra-curricular activities because of her drive and energy.

(Child's name) comes from a practicing Catholic family and is actively involved in the life of *(name of parish)* through her regular service on the altar with her older sister *(name)*, (see enclosure 8 - letter of recommendation from parish priest). As a family, we firmly believe in the tri-partite relationship of home, church and school and, as parents, we are very supportive of our children and actively involved with the school and church communities in which our children are involved. Our desire is for *(Child's name)* to continue her education in a Catholic school as this fully supports the values we hold dear to in our daily lives, and we know *(name of school)* would provide the right nurturing environment for *(Child's name)*'s early adult development.

Example 11 - Academic

Appeal for *(Child's name)* (Date of birth dd/mm/yy)

We wish to appeal against the decision not to offer *(Child's name)* a place at *(name of school)* on the grounds that he did not reach the 111 threshold for entry (score of 108). We appeal on the following academic grounds.

(Child's name) is a very bright and talented boy. He is highly motivated and conscientious in everything he does. *(Child's name)* has performed exceptionally well in both his first school and his current middle school. His school have predicted that he will achieve level 5's in his SATs in all three core subjects with no difficulty at all this year. We expected *(Child's name)* to achieve a much higher score in the 11+ examination than he did and this is why we put *(name of school)* as first choice. *(Child's name)*'s head teacher has had no hesitation in supporting this appeal, as he believes *(name of school)* will be an ideal place for *(Child's name)* to continue his education.

Although we are very pleased *(Child's name)* achieved a good score, we are disappointed because he does not have a place at *(name of school)* . All the indicators showed he would achieve a pass. *(Child's name)* did practise tests in the run up to the examination and scored very high on every single paper. Although *(Child's name)* did *(Child's name)* achieve the required score, we know that he should have passed this examination. *(Child's name)* feels the same way and believes he is well deserving of a grammar school place.

We believe the way in which the Non-verbal Reasoning paper was invigilated did have a direct effect on *(Child's name)*'s score. The paper is divided into two halves (10 minutes are given for each section). Children were not allowed to go forward on the paper, but no specific NFER instructions are to be given with regard to children returning to the first half of the paper if they finish the second half early. Children were routinely going back into the first half of the paper, if they had not completed the questions in this section. These facts have been checked with the chief invigilator at *(name of school)*.

As no specific instructions were given on the issue of being able to 'go back' to section one of the paper, *(Child's name)* understood that he would be able to do this. In fact children in all the other examination rooms were permitted to do this. Unfortunately for *(Child's name)* (wishing always to do the right thing), he put his hand up and asked for clarification on this matter and was told categorically he could not 'go back' by the invigilator. As a result he was forced to leave a portion of the first part of the paper incomplete and sat for some minutes doing absolutely nothing. This particular invigilator gave a ruling on this matter that was not consistent with the instructions given to other children (they had received no such ruling). *(Child's name)* was treated unfairly and disadvantaged in this respect. This did have a bearing on his final score.

If offered a place we believe *(Child's name)* would thrive at *(name of school)* . He would become a valuable member of the *(name of school)* community, just as he is at his current middle school. *(Child's name)* is a member of various clubs and has been popularly elected to be a member of the school council. He is an active participant in the local Catholic community. *(Child's name)* is an enthusiastic member of the young people's choir and a young reader. Father *(name)*, our parish priest, is fully supportive of this appeal as he appreciates the contribution that *(Child's name)* makes to any group he belongs to.

We look forward to hearing from you on the progress of our appeal.

Examples of Appeals

Health Reasons

Example 1 - Health

Appeal for *(Child's name)* **(Date of birth dd/mm/yy)**

We wish to appeal against the decision not to offer *(Child's name)* a grammar school place on the grounds that she did not achieve the required score of 111 (score of 108).

(Child's name) is a very bright child and has achieved excellence across the curriculum in all subjects in her primary school. In year 5 she attained level 5 in maths and high level 4s in both English and Science. *(Child's name)* is expected to achieve level 5 (hopefully 5 star) in all three core subjects in May *(year)*. She is enthusiastic in everything she does and accepts every challenge that presents itself with relish. *(Child's name)* was expected to pass the 11+ examination comfortably and everyone concerned was greatly disappointed and shocked when she did not make the score.

However we believe there are mitigating circumstances and these have directly affected her performance. *(Child's name)* has been quite sick for some time and has been referred to a consultant for investigation at *(name)* Hospital Paediatric wing. She is currently receiving treatment from Dr. *(name)* (Paediatric Consultant) after a diagnosis of *(illness)* (letter enclosed). This is a painful and debilitating condition that causes frequent pain. There are often long periods of time when *(Child's name)* is incapacitated. Obviously, the pressure and stress she felt in facing such an important examination made things worse. During the course of all the 11+ tests, she later told us she felt continual *(body area)* pain and nausea and was repeatedly distracted from the various tasks by this discomfort.

On reflection we believe *(Child's name)* should not have sat the examination on *(date)* as she was not well enough. Initially she seemed a little better on the day and we unadvisedly decided to go ahead with it. We thought she might lose her chance to sit, but later learned that *(Child's name)* could have taken the examination at a later date anyway. *(Child's name)* is still receiving treatment and we expect her medical problem will be under control in the near future. We are convinced that if *(Child's name)* had sat the examination in full health she would have had no difficulty in achieving the required score.

Example 2 - Health

Appeal for *(Child's name)* **(Date of birth dd/mm/yy)**

We wish to appeal against the decision not to offer *(Child's name)* a place at *(name of school)* on the basis that she did not achieve the required score of 111 (score of 109).

(Child's name) is a very bright, hardworking and motivated child. Her primary school have been extremely pleased with her performance since the beginning of her education. In year 5 she did very well in all three core subjects in her SATs. This has led her school to predict she will achieve level 5s in English, Mathematics and Science in May this year (see the head teacher's letter in support of our appeal). We also gave *(Child's name)* some NFER practice tests to do a few weeks before the 11+ examination and she scored over 90% on a regular basis in all three subjects: Verbal Reasoning, Mathematics and Non-verbal Reasoning. For this reason, we believe along with her primary school, that *(Child's name)* should have passed this examination without too much difficulty.

There are some medical factors that had a direct bearing on her performance on the *(date)*. A short while before *(Child's name)* sat the 11+ examination, she suffered a very painful abscess on one of her teeth. She experienced such excruciating pain she had to have time off school. Various treatments failed and finally she had to have the tooth extracted (see the Dentist's report). Naturally she suffered a great deal of discomfort over this period and even after the tooth was extracted. *(Child's name)* found her gums and mouth were very sore for some days and she had difficulty in eating properly.

This whole event was extremely disruptive and distressing and came about at a very crucial time for *(Child's name)*. She lost valuable time both at school and home preparing for the 11+ examination. Before the extraction she found the pain almost unbearable and was not able to work at all. We had planned to revise certain topics with her and go over the practice papers she had done previously, but it was just not possible. We know that when *(Child's name)* entered the examination room, she was neither at her peak academically or in health terms. She was in fact still complaining of soreness and tenderness even after she had sat the examination. On reflection we should not have let her sit the examination at that time, but it is easy to be wise after the event.

(Child's name) only missed the pass mark by a couple of points and we sincerely believe, that had it not been for the above circumstances she would have scored well in excess of 111.

Example 3 - Health

Appeal for *(Child's name)* (Date of birth dd/mm/yy)

We wish to appeal against the decision not to offer *(Child's name)* a *(name of school)* place on the basis that he did nor achieve the required score of 121 (*(Child's name)* scored 108).

(Child's name) is a conscientious, hard-working and intelligent boy. We believe *(Child's name)* will be functioning at level 5 in all three core subjects, by the time of the May SATs this year. His school reports are excellent and his head teacher has been supportive of this appeal. *(Child's name)* is very committed, self-motivated and puts in an immense amount of effort to achieve high standards in every subject area. It was a great disappointment for us to find that *(Child's name)* had not passed the 11+ examination.

There are mitigating circumstances that have a direct bearing on *(Child's name)*'s performance in this examination. *(Child's name)* was involved in a serious car accident when he was five years old and sustained severe whiplash injuries to his neck. This resulted in a chronic muscular condition of the upper back and neck that can only be treated now, with regular physiotherapy. *(Child's name)* is able to take part in normal activities, but has 'ongoing symptoms' (See consultancy report) i.e. he is in constant pain.

As a result, *(Child's name)* finds it difficult to concentrate on written tasks for extended periods. The pain and discomfort he experiences are a continual distraction. A normal writing position for a child requires the neck to be positioned forward and at an angle to the body. This position is extremely difficult for *(Child's name)* but more particularly so, if he needs to hold it over a 50 minute period. In these circumstances it would not be possible for *(Child's name)* to sustain his concentration and be focussed. He would continually need to break away from the paper, to ease the pain in his neck.

The completion of NFER Multiple choice papers requires a high degree of accuracy and attention to detail. The small print on the question paper and the need to fill out boxes on an answer sheet can cause orientation problems if a child is continually interrupted. This is exactly what happened to *(Child's name)*. He continually lost his place on the paper, due to painful distraction and had to spend time finding it again. As a result *(Child's name)* never completed a single paper. This problem was then compounded by a sense of panic. *(Child's name)* told us he look too long to complete each question and as a result felt very distressed in the examination. This increased the likelihood of wrong answers.

When *(Child's name)* completed NFER practice tests at home he scored in excess of 85% every time. However, *(Child's name)* was only able to achieve this when given extra time to make up for minutes lost through painful distraction. *(Child's name)* took a couple of minutes break every now and then to stretch and ease his neck. He was then able to refocus on the paper and complete the tasks. He had no difficulty in doing any of the questions as his understanding examination and technique is excellent.

On reflection, given *(Child's name)*'s medical condition, we should have requested extra time in the examination. However, we only learned afterwards that special provision can be made for children that have 'special needs' (providing this are not related to aptitude). A score of 108 does seem far too low to make an appeal on, but *(Child's name)*'s performance has been severely affected by this condition. *(Child's name)* would have passed the 11+ examination if he had been given another 15 minutes to complete each paper. *(Child's name)* has been seriously disadvantaged in this examination, through no fault of his own and is fully deserving of a grammar school place.

Example 4 - Health

Appeal for *(Child's name)* (Date of birth dd/mm/yy)

We wish to appeal against the decision not to offer *(Child's name)* a grammar school placement on the grounds that she did not achieve the required score of 111 (score of 110).

(Child's name) is of well above average ability, highly motivated and academically capable. She has performed very well throughout the years of the primary schooling and in year 5 achieved high 4/5s in her SAT's in the three core subjects. *(Child's name)* is predicated to achieve straight 5s in English, Mathematics and Science in her Key Stage 2 SATs in May this year In the run-up to the 11+ examination *(Child's name)* was scoring consistently over 85% in all the NFER practice papers in Mathematics, Verbal Reasoning and Non-verbal Reasoning (sample answer sheets enclosed). Both we and her primary school expected *(Child's name)* to pass. We were of course all very disappointed when we discovered that *(Child's name)* had missed the required score by just one mark. *(Child's name)*'s headteacher has had no hesitation in giving her full support to this appeal.

There are some mitigating circumstances that should be taken into account when considering this appeal. Even with all her success. *(Child's name)* has been disadvantaged educationally over a very long period, due to a debilitating medical condition. This has caused her a great deal of physical discomfort, personal disruption and inconvenience. This illness has not only had an overall effect on her educational progress, it has on many occasions caused her not to even function well at the level she has already reached.

For the last five years *(Child's name)* has suffered with a chronic *(illness)*. This causes *(nature of discomfort)*. She is seen regularly by a paediatric consultant at the *(name)* hospital, who is monitoring the condition and prescribing medication to treat it (see consultants letter enclosed).

Obviously this is a very difficult condition for a child to deal with, particularly in a school environment. Her primary school is supportive and *(Child's name)* does have permission to leave the classroom at any point. However, such special arrangements do tend to draw attention to the problem. It has on occasion caused *(Child's name)* social stigma and a great deal of embarrassment with her peers. The medication for this condition is also very strong and does make her ill and tired on a regular basis. She never feels completely well or healthy and has to fight these feelings to accomplish tasks at school and at home. There have been a number of occasions when the condition has just got the better of her and she has failed to attain the expected result.

(Child's name) did well in the 11+ examination, to miss it by only one mark. However we are left thinking; a *(Child's name)* in good health and not significantly disadvantaged by a chronic illness, would have passed this examination with plenty of marks to spare. We believe *(Child's name)* deserves a grammar school place and under normal circumstances would have passed this examination with ease.

Example 5 - Health

Appeal for *(Child's name)* (Date of birth dd/mm/yy)

We wish to appeal against the decision not to offer *(Child's name)* a place at *(name of school)* on the grounds that she did not achieve the required score of 111 (score of 94).

(Child's name) is academically capable, highly motivated and has made consistent improvements in her performance over the last year. Her school is confident she can achieve level 5s in the core subjects of English, Mathematics and Science in the SATs *(year)*. *(Child's name)* had consistently scored over 85% in sample NFER papers (sample multiple choice answer sheets included) and we and her school were confident that she would pass the 11+ comfortably.

Obviously we were very disappointed when *(Child's name)* did not pass the 11+ examination. However, we were very shocked to find *(Child's name)* had scored below 100 points. It did not make sense to us and we knew there had to be a reason for the extremely low score.

Immediately after the examination *(Child's name)* told us that she had been in a great deal of back pain during the tests. On the way to the examination she said the pain was manageable, but it had become far more acute during the examination. She claimed the pain was so bad at one point, she could not think straight. *(Child's name)* does present with severe backache on a regular basis, particularly if she is forced to sit in one position for a long period. *(Child's name)* has had time off school for the problem and has often ended up spending it in bed. Our doctor has been monitoring the condition, so we took *(Child's name)* to see him after the examination for verification (see letter enclosed).

Recently, the problem has flared up again and we are now taking *(Child's name)* to the doctor to obtain a referral to see a paediatric consultant. Given the circumstances it is hardly surprising that *(Child's name)* did so disastrously in the 11+ examination. If we had known that *(Child's name)* was going to have a bout of acute back pain on that day we would have postponed her test. *(Child's name)* usually suffers in silence until she has to say something. If she had at least told us the pain had started we would have turned back from the examination straight away. We are now in a very difficult position, but we are confident of one thing. This score is not truly representative of *(Child's name)*'s ability level and we are hopeful the appeal panel will understand this. No child would have been able to perform at their best or even near their best if they were experiencing such discomfort.

Example 6 - Health

Appeal for *(Child's name)* **(Date of birth dd/mm/yy)**

We wish to appeal against the decision not to offer *(Child's name)* a place at *(name of school)* on the basis that she did not achieve the required score of 117 (score of 115).

(Child's name) is a bright and capable child. She achieved excellent results in all subjects across the curriculum in year five and we are expecting her to do very well in year six. *(Child's name)* is predicted by her school to attain level 5 or 5* in English, Mathematics and Science in her SATs in May this year. *(Child's name)* rarely needs help on any academic tasks, since she is capable and mature enough to work it out on her own. About a month before the 11+ examination *(Child's name)* was scoring over 90% on every NFER practice test in Verbal Reasoning, Non-verbal Reasoning and Mathematics.

As parents we were of course delighted when *(Child's name)* passed the 11+ examination and was granted a grammar school place. However, we believe that under normal circumstances, *(Child's name)* would have easily attained a score in excess of 117. *(Child's name)* regularly suffers from ear, nose and throat allergic reactions. This leads to bouts of asthma, which if coupled with a cold result in serious chest and related infections to the ear and nasal cavities. *(Child's name)* had a number of these attacks in *(year)*, as verified in the doctor's letter. About a week before the 11+ examination, *(Child's name)* had yet another chest and ear infection and was quite poorly. On the day of the examination, she seemed a little better, so we decided to go ahead and let her sit. After, she complained of being quite unwell.

On reflection, we regret allowing *(Child's name)* to sit the examination on *(date)*. However, we were not sure of the procedure permitting children to sit the examination at a later date. We did not want her to miss her chance. We knew it would he very difficult to speak to someone about this problem in the school, on the day of the examination.

(Child's name)'s brother attends *(name of school)* and is doing very well. *(Child's name)* looks up to him and sees him as an example. She has a very close relationship with him and would greatly value his support as she embarks on her secondary education. As parents we are both in full-time employment and work long hours with frequent trips away from home. It will be much easier logistically for us if both children attended the same school.

Example 7 - Health

Appeal for *(Child's name)* (Date of birth dd/mm/yy)

We wish to appeal against the decision not to offer *(Child's name)* a place at *(name of school)* on the grounds that he did not achieve the required score of 111 (score of 106).

(Child's name) is a very able child with outstanding academic ability. He is conscientious and highly motivated in all he does. If *(Child's name)* is informed about the need to improve in any area, he immediately takes this on board and actively seeks to make the necessary change. He is very enthusiastic about writing and last year had one of his poems selected for publication in the *(name)* anthology. This was as a result of his work being selected from among thousands of other entries in the 8-11 Young Writers Poetry Competition. Due to *(Child's name)*'s exceptional performance in both year 5 and 6 his school expect him to achieve level 5 or 5* in English, Mathematics and Science in his SATs in May this year.

(Child's name) gives of his best in everything. His teacher's regard him as a mature student who always acts as an excellent role model for his peers. He continually involves himself in extra-curricular activities; he recently assisted in the school office by answering the telephone and dealing with visitors and he also took a leading role in helping out at the school fair.

We were very surprised when *(Child's name)* failed to achieve the required score, as he was expected by all concerned to pass the examination with ease. *(Child's name)*'s headteacher had no hesitation in immediately lending full support to this appeal, as he believes *(Child's name)*'s score is not truly reflective of his ability level. This is borne out by the fact that he was consistently scoring over 90% in NFER practice tests in the run-up to the examination.

On reflection, we believe that *(Child's name)* should not have sat the examination on *(date)* as he was suffering from a very heavy cold and flu symptoms. He was too ill to go to school on *(day)* and was given medicine throughout the day to ease the symptoms. We contemplated taking him to the doctor, but thought we would wait to see if his condition improved. Initially he seemed a little better on the day of the test and against our better judgement we decided to let him sit. We were also persuaded by the fact that *(Child's name)* was very nervous and worried about the examination and wanted to get it over and done with.

Afterwards, on the way home, *(Child's name)* told us he felt extremely unwell throughout the examination and found it hard to concentrate and focus on what he was doing. He knew he had not done as well as he should and felt he might not get through. Obviously, we now regret the decision to let him sit as we can clearly see his unhealthy state adversely affected his performance.

(Child's name) is very close to his sister *(name)* who joined *(name of school)* last September. We were very much hoping that this very closeness could be maintained and further strengthened by *(Child's name)* attending the same school. We believe *(Child's name)* is fully deserving of a grammar school place and under normal circumstances would have passed the examination without difficulty.

Example 8 - Health

Appeal for *(Child's name)* (Date of birth dd/mm/yy)

We wish to appeal against the decision not to offer *(Child's name)* a place at *(name of school)* on the grounds that she did not reach the 111 threshold for entry (*(Child's name)* scored 107).

(Child's name) is a highly motivated, intelligent and academically capable child, as well being conscientious in everything she does. *(Child's name)* has performed exceptionally well in primary school, impressing her teachers with a high level of dedication and a phenomenal work rate. As mentioned on the enclosed school letter *(Child's name)* has been praised for her confidence in Maths, being articulate in English and has a naturally inquisitive mind in Science, leading her to asking mature questions.

We have received strong support for this appeal from the head teacher who realises her full potential and is exceptionally confident that *(Child's name)* will achieve level 5 in Key Stage Two SATs, in all three core subjects without any difficulty. *(Child's name)* was also scoring consistently 85% and over in her practice NFER papers, which indicated she would pass without any problem. *(Child's name)* did feel confident that she would pass and was obviously very disappointed as we all were when the results came through.

We believe there are specific health issues that directly affected *(Child's name)*'s chances of passing the 11+ examination. Attached is a letter from *(Child's name)*'s doctor, stating that she suffers from recurrent attacks of an upper respiratory tract infection (wheezy attack) and nose bleeds for which she has an appointment on *(date)*. *(Child's name)* did have flu symptoms a couple of days before the examination that triggered the associated symptoms described above. As a result, she suffered a serious wheezy attack, whilst leaving school on Friday, the day before the examination. *(Child's name)* was quite distressed, as the symptoms persisted until we arrived home. We did not take her to the doctor's surgery as we had the inhalers at home, which we administered as soon as we arrived. We waited to see if she responded to the medication before taking her to the doctors. She was feeling a bit better after the medication and we did not want to waste any of her time as she had the examination the following day and she needed time to compose herself for the examination.

Although the acute symptoms subsided, *(Child's name)* then faced the aftermath of the attack. When these attacks occur it takes *(Child's name)* more than a day to recover. There is resulting lethargy, weakness and tiredness, which means *(Child's name)* finds it very difficult to concentrate and focus on academic tasks.

(Child's name) was still feeling this way on Saturday, the day of the examination, but we thought that she had no choice but to sit. However, we were not sure if there was a procedure permitting children to sit the examination at a later date and we did not want her to miss her chance. We now realise, through discussion with other parents, whose children sat the examination that we could have postponed it until later. As a result, we deeply regret the decision we made in allowing *(Child's name)* to sit the examination. It is now clear to us that *(Child's name)* did not have the best chance to demonstrate her ability, due the symptoms she was experiencing.

(Child's name) is diligent, enthusiastic and displays a level of maturity rarely found in someone so young. She is very ambitious and determined to reach her full potential. We believe *(name of school)* will best facilitate this and had *(Child's name)*'s health been better on the day we are certain she would have secured a pass without difficulty.

31

Example 9 - Health

Appeal for *(Child's name)* **(Date of birth dd/mm/yy)**

We wish to appeal against the decision not to offer *(Child's name)* a place at *(name of school)* on the grounds that he did not achieve the required score.

(Child's name) is academically capable, highly motivated and has made consistent improvements in his performance over the last year. *(name of current school)* are very confident he can achieve level 5's in the core subjects of English, Mathematics and Science in the SATs this year. *(Child's name)* is in the top sets for all his subjects. He is currently doing Year 7 work in his Maths class, as the material that is normally given out is not challenging enough for him. He is at the very top of his class. All his teachers are pleased with his progress and believe him to be of very high ability.

It is abundantly clear from *(Child's name)*'s academic record that he was able to pass this examination. There is a very specific reason why *(Child's name)* failed to achieve the required score. A clear and concise account of what happened on the day will suffice.

(Child's name) was dropped off at *(name of school)* at 8:30am for the 11+ examination. At this point he appeared to be his usual self and even during the forty-five minute wait before the examination commenced he says he felt okay. The examination began at 9.15am and *(Child's name)* related to us that he started to feel ill at about 9:25am with a headache, high temperature and dizziness. This rapidly progressed to blurring of vision and trembling over the next fifteen minutes resulting in him feeling very ill. He struggled on with the Maths paper thinking he would not be given permission to stop once he had started. When the break came he felt too weak to stand. *(Child's name)* should have told the teacher how awful he was feeling at this point, but we all know children do not have the wisdom of adults and neither should they be blamed for it.

He told us that by the time the English examination commenced he felt even worse. His overriding thoughts were now dominated by wanting the exam to end so he could be sick. During the English written paper he felt like vomiting and immediately after the examination *(Child's name)* was sick in the toilets. Orange juice and chocolate biscuits were given during the break which exacerbated his symptoms of nausea. The teachers had obviously become aware of how ill *(Child's name)* felt and placed a bucket by his exam desk before the Verbal Reasoning exam started.

We believe that the teachers responsible for invigilating the examination should have taken action at this point and pulled *(Child's name)* out of the room. They obviously knew how ill he was if they were even prepared to allow him to be sick in the examination room. We should have been called and told to collect *(Child's name)*. It was very unfair to allow *(Child's name)* to continue under the circumstances when it was obvious he would not be able to perform at his best.

The teacher's expectations were fulfilled; as immediately *(Child's name)* had completed the Verbal Reasoning paper he was violently sick before he could leave the examination room. The only comment made on the exam paper was the word 'sick'. This in no way described how ill *(Child's name)* had become. Those invigilating the examination were perfectly aware of *(Child's name)*'s condition immediately following the English exam and before the Verbal Reasoning exam commenced. The fact is they did not act correctly and this has led to *(Child's name)* to under-achieve in the exam. His attempt should have been made null and void and a new examination date set.

When we returned to collect *(Child's name)* we were very surprised to find him in the state he was. Particularly as no attempt had been made to notify us of his condition. He was very pale and weak. We had to lead by hand to the car, as he was barely able to walk; a far cry from the normal *(Child's name)*, who is athletic and full of energy. When we found out a bucket had been placed by his desk, we were astonished. Why had the invigilators allowed him to continue? It was clearly ridiculous to expect a child to concentrate under such circumstances.

(Child's name) has always impressed us with his determination to success even when circumstances are against him. This led him to valiantly continue when his performance was considerably compromised. The marks he achieved bear no relationship to his ability level. We are extremely disappointed and feel he has been treated very unfairly. A child cannot be expected to make decisions over whether to continue or not in an examination. The invigilator of the examination should have acted *(Child's name)*'s best interest and clearly failed to do so.

On a more positive note: there are excellent facilities at *(name of school)* for sport and *(Child's name)* would thrive in this environment. *(Child's name)* is not only academically able; he loves all sports and is particularly good at cycling. Over the past year he has won numerous gold medals and trophies. In *(year)* he won the *(name of event)* for his age category. The event was televised and *(Child's name)* appeared on television.

If offered a place, *(Child's name)* would thrive at *(name of school)*. He is enthusiastic, dedicated and determined to reach his true potential.

Examples of Appeals

Circumstantial Reasons

Example - 1 - Circumstantial

Appeal for *(Child's name)* and *(Child's name)* (Date of birth dd/mm/yy)

We wish to appeal against the decision not to offer our twin daughters, *(Child's name)* and *(Child's name)* places at *(name of school)* on the grounds that they did not achieve the required score of 111 (*(Child's name)* scored 104 and *(Child's name)* scored 102).

Both *(Child's name)* and *(Child's name)* are very bright girls with considerable academic ability. Last year they excelled in all subjects across the curriculum and did particularly well in English, Mathematics and Science. According to recent reports from their school both *(Child's name)* and *(Child's name)* are expected to achieve level 5 or 5* in all three core subjects at Key Stage 2 SATs in May of this year. Both children had done a series of NFER practice tests in the weeks prior to the exam and both had consistently scored over 85% in Verbal Reasoning, Non-verbal Reasoning and Mathematics. Both we and their school expected them to pass the 11+ examination comfortably. We can only conclude that the tragic events that were unfolding on the very day of the examination had a serious affect on both girls and led them to significantly underachieve.

During the summer of last year, my sister, and aunt to our two children was taken seriously ill with *(illness)*. Treatment persisted throughout *(month)* and *(month)* of *(year)*, but there was no significant improvement in her condition. On *(date)* she was taken seriously ill again and admitted to hospital for *(treatment)*. By *(date)* her condition had deteriorated and she was taken into intensive care with her life in the balance. Sadly she passed away during the morning of *(date)*, whilst the children were actually sitting the 11+ examination.

The twins were very close to their aunty *(name)*, who incidentally was only *(age)* years old when she died, They were taken to visit her three times a week over the long period of her illness. During the week before the examination the children were taken to the hospital on the *(date)* and *(date)* for visits. They could see that their aunty was very ill and were so upset about this they had to he taken out of the ward. There was a very tense atmosphere in the home and everybody sensed she might die. There were phone calls day and night and nobody could think about anything but aunty *(name)*. Most poignantly, one of the very last things she gave to the twins was her promise to attend their birthday party on *(date)*, the day after the examination. Sadly, she was never to see that day and ever since the twins have been devastated by her loss.

We believe that both *(Child's name)* and *(Child's name)* were so affected by these traumatic events that they were unable to give of their best on the day of the examination. To be honest their heart was not in it. They did not even want to go to sit the examination and felt they should be at the hospital. They later told us they found it very hard to concentrate on what they were doing in the examination. All they could think about was aunty *(name)* and whether or not she would live.

On reflection we should cancelled their examination, but at the time we were not sure whether they would he given another chance to sit. It was difficult to make sensible decisions in such dire and tragic circumstances. When the results came through we of course regretted letting them sit. However, we truly believe that under normal circumstances, both *(Child's name)* and *(Child's name)* would have comfortably passed the 11+ examination.

Example 2 - Circumstantial

Appeal for *(Child's name)* (Date of birth dd/mm/yy)

We wish to appeal against the decision not to offer our son *(Child's name)* a place at *(name of school)* on the grounds that he did not achieve the required pass score of 117 (score of 103).

(Child's name) is a very able child who has demonstrated he is well above average academically. At his current school he is regularly tested on an internal basis and consistently achieves high grades in all subject areas. As an all-rounder he is very good at most sports and shows considerable talent musically. *(Child's name)*'s NFER scores clearly show that he is of above average ability (overall score of 124). In particular his mathematics score (130) and his reading score (140) show him to be well above average in these two areas of study. We have also included a report from *(Child's name)*'s headteacher to substantiate his academic ability. She is fully supportive of our appeal and believes as we do, that *(Child's name)* should have passed the 11+ examination with ease.

It is difficult to explain why *(Child's name)* did not perform well. All the indicators suggested he should have passed the 11+ examination. In NFER practice tests he was consistently achieving over 90% in the run-up to the examination. As his score is quite low, we can only conclude that what occurred immediately prior to the examination must have unsettled him and caused him to significantly underachieve.

He was very concerned, as we all were about his grandmother who became ill with a very high temperature on the evening of the *(date)* (the day before the exam). She is quite frail and in her 80's, so this was a very worrying development. As we are her primary carers and she lives with us, this caused a great deal of disruption in the house. The high level of anxiety led to some family arguments about *(Child's name)*'s drop off/collection arrangements with regard to the examination. As a result *(Child's name)* went to bed very late and then could not sleep for worrying. He complained of being very tired in the morning before we set off with him for the examination. We believe these circumstances seriously affected *(Child's name)*'s performance on the day.

(Child's name) has a brother at *(name of school)* and their relationship is quite close. It will help *(Child's name)* a great deal, in his transition from primary to secondary school to have the support and encouragement of his brother. We believe *(Child's name)* is deserving of a grammar school place and under normal circumstances would have achieved a very high score.

Example 3 - Circumstantial

Appeal for *(Child's name)* (Date of birth dd/mm/yy)

We wish to appeal against the decision not to offer *(Child's name)* a grammar school place on the basis that he did not achieve the required score of 111 ((C*hild's name)* scored 107).

(Child's name) is a conscientious, hard-working and intelligent boy. This is reflected in his CAT and SATs scores in English, Mathematics and Science. We believe that *(Child's name)* will achieve level 5 in all three core subjects in the May SATs. He has also performed excellently in ICT, French and Spanish. We were extremely pleased with *(Child's name)*'s mid-term report in which he was commended by his teachers for his excellent progress.

(Child's name) is committed, self-motivated and puts in an immense amount of effort to achieve high standards. He reads widely of his own volition and uses reference books and the internet for research purposes in an intelligent and methodical way. *(Child's name)* recently gained a silver award for a project on famous people.

(Child's name) should have passed the 11+ examination. A few weeks before *(Child's name)* sat the examination we gave him NFER practice papers to do in Verbal Reasoning, Mathematics and Non-verbal Reasoning. He achieved over 85% on all of these papers. We have provided some sample answer sheets as evidence of this fact (see enclosed). This led us to believe that *(Child's name)* would pass this examination comfortably. We were extremely surprised and disappointed when *(Child's name)* failed to achieve the required score.

We know *(Child's name)* significantly underachieved on the day of the examination and can only conclude that the less than ideal circumstances that he had to endure at that time contributed to this. His grandfather, who lives with us, had a bout of very serious illness that could have been fatal in the fortnight before the examination. This initially required emergency hospital treatment and then nursing care at home. We were all very worried about the sudden deterioration in his health, and this especially affected *(Child's name)*, who is very close to his grandfather. Our family life was much disrupted, with the need for an organised care regime and the many visits and phone calls from well wishing relatives.

(Child's name) was increasingly distracted by what was happening at the time and we did notice that he was having trouble completing homework. In the week before the examination *(Child's name)* did a few more practice tests and there were more mistakes on the papers than usual. When we went through these things with him afterwards, we realised he understood everything perfectly well. We can only assume that while he was doing these tests he was unfocussed and his mind was not fully engaged on the task.

On the day of the examination *(Child's name)* did not really want to go and said he did not feel ready. We just thought it was nerves, but on reflection we now realise that *(Child's name)* was under considerable emotional strain and very anxious about his grandfather. He was not functioning at his best and the examination result sadly reflects this fact. We should have delayed the examination for *(Child's name)* until this crisis was over, in the hope everything would soon return to normal. We deeply regret this decision as we know *(Child's name)* would have passed under normal circumstances and fully deserves a grammar school place.

Example 4 - Circumstantial

Appeal for *(Child's name)* (Date of birth dd/mm/yy)

We wish to appeal against the decision not to offer *(Child's name)* a grammar school place on the grounds that she did not achieve the required score of 111 (*(Child's name)* scored 101).

(Child's name) is a very bright, academically capable and well motivated child. She has performed very well throughout her primary schooling. There is a very good prospect she will achieve level 5s in all three core subjects in May this year, as the letter from her head teacher attests. *(Child's name)* scored consistently over 90% in all the NFER practice tests that she completed some weeks before sitting the 11+ examination. Everybody expected *(Child's name)* to pass the examination and we are all shocked at the result. The score suggests she badly underachieved on the day of the examination. We know this performance is not reflective of her ability level. *(Child's name)* should have passed by a comfortable margin.

We can only conclude that events taking place at the time *(Child's name)* sat the examination had a serious impact on her performance. *(Child's name)* is a very quiet and demure child who says very little about what is troubling her. She tends to withdraw when there are problems and difficulties rather than talk about them. About a week before the examination a very close friend of our family died suddenly. He was a very frequent visitor to our house and *(Child's name)* was very fond of him. She regarded him as an uncle as he spent more time with our family than his own.

His tragic death affected us all, but *(Child's name)* in her customary way did not share how she was feeling. We knew *(Child's name)* was very upset about this as nobody close to her had ever died before. We tried to function normally as a family, so that it would not affect her preparation for the examination. The funeral took place on the morning *(Child's name)* took the 11+ examination. We knew she was thinking about this as we drove her to the school. While *(Child's name)* was sitting the examination, we left to go to the funeral. This must have been on her mind as she tried to concentrate on the various tests. *(Child's name)* seemed visibly upset when we picked her up from the school after we returned from the funeral. She told us that she did not think she had done as well as she could have done. We then realised we had made a mistake in letting *(Child's name)* sit. Obviously we said nothing and hoped for the best.

On reflection we believe it would have been better if *(Child's name)* had not sat the 11+ examination on that day. However, it is easy to be wise after the event. During that week the family was in the grip of bereavement and it was hard to think straight. Although *(Child's name)* did not talk about her feelings, she was grieving as much as the rest of the family and our attempts to protect her from the effects of this tragic death were sadly misplaced. We now know it would have been far more beneficial for her, if she had come to the funeral and said goodbye to her friend. She had asked us about the funeral arrangements and we now realise she wanted to come. This would have been painful but it would have started the grieving process earlier. *(Child's name)* is still not talking about what happened, and we know this is the first stage of the healing process. Her lack of success in the examination has made this even harder, as we are sure it must have occurred to her, that what happened seriously affected her performance on the day. We believe that *(Child's name)* is deserving of a grammar school place. If she had sat the 11+ examination under normal circumstances she would have passed.

Example 5 - Circumstantial

Appeal for *(Child's name)* **(Date of birth dd/mm/yy)**

In the three months previous to *(Child's name)* sitting for 11+, my husband was diagnosed with cancer. The diagnosis was officially given on *(date)* and soon after he underwent a serious operation. This was followed up by Chemotherapy on *(date)*. He is still off work, awaiting scans, further tests and appointments.

This has been very traumatic for the family and [documentary evidence supplied] particularly *(Child's name)* who is very close to his father. *(Child's name)* has not been made aware of all the details of the situation but as a very intelligent child has worked it out for himself. He has no doubt been thinking he could lose his father, although this possibility has not been discussed openly. We are of course hopeful there will be a favourable outcome to the treatment.

(Child's name) has not been himself since the diagnosis. He has been listless and his attention span is brief. He does not appear to concentrate on things at all. This was particularly worrying in the run-up to the 11+ examination. We know he was capable of passing this exam, given his performance in practice papers previous to the diagnosis. However there was a marked deterioration in the run-up to the examination. We were shocked that he achieved a low score, but were hardly surprised given the circumstances.

We believe *(Child's name)* is an able, intelligent child who should be given the opportunity of a grammar school education. It is very unfortunate that such a traumatic thing should have happened so close to the examination and we feel sure he could have passed if things had been normal at home.

Example 6 - Circumstantial

Appeal for *(Child's name)* (Date of birth dd/mm/yy)

We wish to appeal against the decision not to offer our son *(Child's name)* a grammar school place on the grounds that he did not achieve the required score of 111 (score of 107).

(Child's name) is very intelligent, academically capable and is driven to succeed in everything he does. His school work in year 5 is evidence of this, as he attained high level 4s in all three core subjects in his SATs. His teacher informed us that all his independent projects were the best in his entire class as they were of such an outstanding quality. *(Child's name)*'s ICT skills are also very advanced. He recently gave a power-point presentation on a voluntary basis at school that impressed everybody and received a very high commendation. This involved the complex process of using hyperlinks to on-line research articles. *(Child's name)* has recently been elected as Chairman for the School Council where he has the responsibility of liaising with staff and pupils about issues of concern. *(Child's name)* is an all-rounder and excels in everything he does, which made his failure to achieve a pass score in the 11+ examination very hard to take.

We along with his school are confident he will achieve level 5 or 5* in English, Mathematics and Science in his SATs in May this year. About a month before the examination *(Child's name)* did a series of NFER practice papers and consistently scored over 85% on Verbal Reasoning, Non-verbal Reasoning and Mathematics.

It is clear to all concerned that *(Child's name)* should have passed the 11+ examination We believe there are specific circumstances that led to his failure to attain a pass score on the day. Firstly, *(Child's name)* was still feeling unwell after he had been suffering from a fever and an upset stomach. His general low state of health gave rise to and was compounded by frequent asthmatic attacks and a persistent and irritating cough. He had been to see the doctor the day before the examination who prescribed antibiotics and more asthma inhalers. Secondly, *(Child's name)* was badly affected emotionally by the sudden death of his aunt only a week before. *(Child's name)* had a very close relationship with her and he was so upset that he had to have time off school to recover. His father also had to spend some time away from the family home to conduct the cultural funeral rites. This added to *(Child's name)*'s depression as he felt less supported. This was crucial as the 11+ examination was only a few days away. The bereavement has left the whole family in a state of shock and sadness. *(Child's name)* was very much looking forward to his baptism at church and this had to be cancelled too.

On reflection it would have been better if *(Child's name)* had not sat the 11+ examination on *(date)* given such dire circumstances. However he was adamant that he wished to go ahead with it and we unfortunately went along with his decision despite our misgivings. In typical fashion *(Child's name)* thought he would be letting people down and running away from his responsibility if he did not sit the examination on that day. We have of course regretted the decision ever since, but as the family was very distraught and in the midst of bereavement we were perhaps not thinking straight.

(Child's name) is deserving of a grammar school placement and under normal circumstances would have comfortably passed the 11+ examination. He is aspiring to follow in the footsteps of his three elder sisters who have all been to the same grammar school, which is a very convenient distance from our home.

Example 7 - Circumstantial

Appeal for *(Child's name)* **(Date of birth dd/mm/yy)**

We wish to appeal against the decision not to offer *(Child's name)* a place at *(name of school)* on the following grounds:

(Child's name) is a bright, highly motivated and academically able child. He is expected to achieve level 5 in all three core subjects in his SATs tests in May this year. We have supplied a letter from his current school showing his recent test performances and an independent assessment conducted last year to gauge *(Child's name)*'s suitability for a grammar school education. This information clearly shows that *(Child's name)* is a very capable and intelligent boy who should do very well in a grammar school.

(Child's name)'s twin brother *(name)* has already been given a place at *(name of school)*. Both twins' ability levels are virtually identical although they have different interests and strengths. *(Child's name)* has achieved very similar results to *(name)* in grammar selection tests, school tests, music exams and sporting activities.

As parents we cannot conceive of separating them at this point as we have always treated both boys in an even handed and fair way. We believe it would be psychologically damaging for both *(child's name)* and *(name)* as they are such close friends and are never apart. It would also seriously affect *(child's name)*'s self esteem if forced and unwelcome distinction be drawn between them at this stage. They know themselves there is virtually no difference in their ability levels. Both *(Child's name)* and *(name)* would perceive such a distinction to be unfair and they would be right in making this assumption.

There is no difference in the musical abilities of the two twins except that *(Child's name)* has a slight hearing disability. In assessing *(Child's name)*'s musical aptitude the examiners will not have been aware that he has had hearing difficulties since early childhood. Although he has largely overcome these problems, he may have been disadvantaged in the newly designed hearing test. He is however, like his brother functioning at Grade 4 on the piano and would he quite willing to play a piece to demonstrate his musical ability.

For obvious logistical reasons we wish the twins to attend the same school. As there is a younger brother too it would he extremely difficult if all three children attended different schools.

We believe *(Child's name)* is as deserving as *(name)* in being granted a grammar school place. Both twins will be a worthy asset to your school.

Example 8 - Circumstantial

Appeal for *(Child's name)* (Date of birth dd/mm/yy)

1 am appealing against the decision not to offer my daughter *(Child's name)* a grammar school place at *(name of school)*.

(Child's name) is a high achiever who has attained academic excellence in all areas of the curriculum. She is in the top sets for Mathematics and English and is predicted to score level 5s in all three-core subjects in her SATs in May *(year)*. At a recent parents evening, *(Child's name)*'s class teacher lavished praise upon her and assured us she would flourish and excel in a grammar school environment. *(Child's name)* is a child of outstanding ability, so we were not surprised at this confirmation of her potential.

There have been times recently however when *(Child's name)* has under achieved, particularly when nerves have got the better of her. We believe that the panic and extreme nervousness, which she seems to experience is related to a series of traumas she has been subjected to over the last year. Before this time she was a happy and contented little girl with lots of confidence. What happened to change all this?

As a result of systematic bullying and repeated victimisation over a very long period, we had no alternative but to move *(Child's name)* to another school in *(year)*. In *(year)*, *(Child's name)* was referred to a paediatric specialist for repeated bouts of *(illness)*. He concluded that the incidents at school were the cause of the problem. Throughout *(year)* *(Child's name)* was repeatedly seen by the G.P. to receive treatment for stress related illnesses, as a direct result of the bullying. The situation became so severe by *(date)* and *(Child's name)* became so ill that we had to withdraw her from the school. She is still very nervous and over sensitive. Getting used to a new school has been difficult for *(Child's name)*. In one moment she lost all the friends she had and has not only needed to regain her confidence, but make new friends too.

This was further compounded by the migration of my sister and her family to *(country)* in *(month)*. *(Child's name)* has lost her favourite aunt and was very upset about this. She still talks about it and misses her, but visiting *(country)* is out of the question financially.

(Child's name) is getting back to normal gradually, but the 11+ examination was a traumatic experience for her. Under normal circumstances she would have passed comfortably.

As a family, we are practising Catholics who fully participate in the life of the parish. We are very keen for *(Child's name)* to have a Catholic education, particularly one that is fitted to her academic ability. We believe that *(name of school)* will nurture *(Child's name)*, spiritually, emotionally and educationally. *(Child's name)*'s brother *(name)* is already at *(name of school)* in year 8. *(Child's name)* is close to her brother and was very much looking forward to joining him next September. The practicalities of getting two children to different schools will be extremely difficult. Although we live in *(town)*, *(name of school)* is in fact our nearest Catholic School.

We would fully support *(name of school)* and we know *(Child's name)* would participate in many after school activities. *(Child's name)* is very competitive and loves being involved in sport and music in her current school. She is determined to succeed in everything she does despite the setbacks.

We look forward to hearing from you on the progress of *(Child's name)*'s appeal.

Example 9 - Circumstantial

Appeal for *(Child's name)* **(Date of birth dd/mm/yy)**

We wish to appeal against the decision not to offer our daughter, *(Child's name)* a place at *(name of school)* on the grounds that she did not achieve the required score of 111. *(Child's name)* scored 101.

(Child's name) is a very bright, committed, conscientious individual with considerable academic ability. *(Child's name)* is tested regularly at her current school and consistently achieves high grades in Maths, English, and Science, whilst also showing considerable talent in other subjects, specifically music and dance. Recent discussions with subject tutors from her school have indicated that she is expected to achieve level 5 in all three core subjects at Key Stage 2 SATs in May this year. All indicators prior to the exams had suggested that *(Child's name)* would comfortably pass the 11+ examination. *(Child's name)* completed a series of practice papers prior to sitting the exams and always passed these comfortably, consistently scoring over 85% in all NFER Verbal Reasoning, Non-verbal Reasoning and Maths test papers.

We can only conclude that the tragic events that had unfolded a few weeks before the exams traumatically affected *(Child's name)*, causing her to under-perform significantly.

At 1.15am on *(date)*, my wife and I woke to find that part of our home was ablaze. The fire had burnt through our electricity supply and telephone cables. We therefore had to try to escape from our home with the children, in complete darkness whilst avoiding poisoness smoke. Once outside the house we could see the severity of the fire. The flames at this point had reached the first floor melting the windows, and several trees close to the house were fully ablaze. The whole family was extremely shaken up by this near death experience.

We lost over 25% of the house with the remainder being smoked damaged. The family was then forced to spend the next four weeks living in a shared single room in a hotel. *(Child's name)* completed her last NFER practise test paper sitting on the edge of the bed at the hotel. Our family moved back into the home approximately four weeks after the fire, but we were forced to move back out again as the house was still not habitable, adding additional distress and disruption to the family. Each member of the family lost a significant number of personal possessions. *(Child's name)* however lost significantly more than other members. All of her books were destroyed and her toys were burnt including her favourite doll. *(Child's name)*'s CD collection melted and many items of her clothing were fire damaged and beyond repair.

After the fire it was difficult to organise many more practise tests for *(Child's name)*, due to the significant disruption to family life. *(Child's name)* was also very emotional and distressed, finding it very difficult to concentrate. This is supported by the fact that she lost weight, dropping a whole size in clothes. She was also very withdrawn and occasionally 'bed wetted', which has never been a problem for her previously.

(Child's name) has found it difficult to sleep since the fire, having nightmares about the fire reoccurring and what might happen if we did not all get out the next time.

This behaviour shows she has bottled up many of her feelings, as she has not readily talked about these events. In her characteristic way, she recently commented that she had not talked openly before, because "Mummy and Daddy already had enough to worry about". It is clear that her failure to achieve the score everyone expected in her 11+ exams is as a direct result of this tragic life changing event. *(Child's name)*'s doctor has diagnosed that she is suffering from post traumatic stress as a result of the fire and has consequently referred her for counselling. A copy of the GP's letter is enclosed for reference.

On reflection we should have cancelled her exam. However at the time we thought that rescheduling the exam would be even more disruptive. With the benefit of hindsight we have appreciated how traumatised our daughter really was. Our failure to fully grasp this is due to the fact that the whole family was in a state of shock. It is difficult to think and act rationally and decisively when there are so many practical problems that need to be urgently addressed.

On receiving the results we realised that we had made a mistake in allowing her to sit the exam at that time, as *(Child's name)* had been significantly affected. We truly believe however that if *(Child's name)* had been given the opportunity to sit the exams under normal circumstances she would have comfortably passed the 11 + examination.

Example 10 - Circumstantial

Appeal for *(Child's name)* **(Date of birth dd/mm/yy)**

We wish to appeal against the decision not to offer *(Child's name)* a place at a grammar school, because he did not achieve the required score (scored 114).

(Child's name) is highly motivated and conscientious in everything he does. He is predicted to achieve high level 5s in all three core subjects in his SATs next May. While preparing for the 11 + in September he scored over 90% in practice papers for verbal reasoning. *(Child's name)*'s head teacher had no hesitation in fully supporting this appeal, as he believes *(Child's name)* to be a bright child who is deserving of a grammar school placement.

All the indicators suggested that *(Child's name)* should have achieved a higher score in the 11+ examination than he did, and that is why we have no hesitation in putting *(name of school)* as our first choice of school. At first we were very surprised *(Child's name)* failed to achieve the required score, but on reflection, it is hardly surprising, given the circumstances he found himself subjected to. *(Child's name)* knew there was intense competition for limited places and his anxiety about the examination was reflected in remarks he made on the day and night before. He was uncharacteristically nervous of what the result might be, as he seemed to sense that he was not performing at his best. We clearly believe the final breakdown of our marriage had a direct bearing on *(Child's name)*'s performance in the 11+ examination.

We divorced in October, just before the 11+ examination. This has been very unsettling for *(Child's name)* as the youngest child and he has shown signs of insecurity and emotional stress which has resulted in an erratic academic performance. Lately, he has become a nervous and rather withdrawn child saying very little. He has shown less interest in his hobbies and finds it more difficult to get down to important tasks. Before he never lacked enthusiasm or determination in any area. No doubt the personal circumstances our family has undergone have contributed to this. As neither his behaviour or recent performance is typical, we can only conclude our recent divorce was a major reason for his failure to attain his best in the 11+ examination.

Although we separated only on a trial basis just over a year ago, *(Child's name)* was very hopeful the rift would be mended and we would be a family once again. As a result he has been very depressed and unduly subdued in his moods recently. On occasion there have been extreme outbursts of anger and crying for apparently no reason. We have noted this and if it continues we may consider some counselling to help him cope with the effects of our breakdown in marriage. Due to family circumstances and distance regular contact with his mother has also been more restricted and this has added to his distress. The constant efforts of wider members of the family of which he was aware, to re-unite us has also probably given *(Child's name)* false hope and made our final decision to divorce even more devastating.

46

(Child's name) has rarely shown signs of happiness and contentment since *(month)* last year. His ability to focus on a task and concentrate was severely affected in the weeks after the divorce proceedings. There was a definite deterioration in his performance prior to the examination, which we found difficult to understand at the time, but on reflection it is perfectly understandable. The tension in our fractured relationship has unfortunately and to our regret, inevitably swamped the needs of our child, for support and understanding. Only time will heal this, but of course we are now concerned about the short-term.

(Child's name)'s brother already attends *(name of school)*. He is now in year 9 and performing well. We believe he will be his mentor, easing his transition from junior to secondary school. As we live in the school catchment, they will be able to travel to school together. This will be of great support to *(Child's name)* in the current circumstances.

Currently *(Child's name)* enjoys sports and has been a keen member of the school football and handball teams and participated in athletic events last year, which he thoroughly enjoyed. We hope this interest will be further developed throughout his secondary education and we know *(name of school)* has excellent facilities. *(Child's name)* is self-disciplined, has demonstrated he can work on his own and with others, always compliant, loves a challenge and is popular with both peers and adults alike.

At present *(Child's name)*'s self esteem and confidence have been affected by his family circumstances. He feels he has worked hard and does not understand why he did not achieve the pass mark which was always predicted. Given time *(Child's name)* will overcome the personal trauma that produced this setback. He will soon learn to thrive and excel again and be able reach his true potential and that is why we believe a grammar school education is right and proper for *(Child's name)*.

Please find enclosed a copy of the decree absolute and headmaster's appeal submission in support of our appeal.

Example 11 - Circumstantial

Appeal for *(Child's name)* **(Date of birth dd/mm/yy)**

We wish to appeal against the decision not to offer our daughter *(Child's name)* a place at *(name of school)* on the grounds that she did not achieve the required pass score of 111 (score of 107).

(Child's name) is very intelligent and an academically able child. Her schoolwork in year 5 is evidence of this, as she attained level 4's in all three core subjects in SATs. We believe that *(Child's name)* will achieve level 5 in all three core subjects in the May SATs. *(Child's name)* consistently scored over 90% in all the core NFER practice papers that she completed some weeks before sitting the 11+ examination and we are all shocked at the result. The score suggests she badly underachieved on the day of the exam. We know this performance is not reflective of her ability. *(Child's name)* should have passed by a comfortable margin.

We can only conclude the events taking place prior to sitting the examination had a serious impact on her performance. On the *(date)* (less than a week before *(Child's name)* sat the 11+ exam) the family including *(Child's name)* attended our aunts' funeral (death certificate attached as appendix 1). Although she was suffering from cancer for a long time, the doctors had given the all clear after intensive chemotherapy on two occasions; therefore it was a shock to us all when they told us she only had couple of days to live. *(Child's name)* took this very badly and withdrew emotionally. She also had difficulty sleeping during the week leading up to 11+. *(Child's name)* was very close to her aunty *(name)* from a young age, who incidentally was only *(age)* when she died. On the day of the 11+ we had planned weeks before that we would visit aunt *(name)* after *(Child's name)* had completed the exam. *(Child's name)* had said she did not feel ready and able to focus on the day of the examination; this must have been on her mind as she tried to concentrate on the tests. *(Child's name)* seemed visibly upset when we picked her up from school after the exam. She told us she did not think she had done as well as she could have, and kept asking why the doctors could not save her aunty.

We then realised we made the mistake in letting *(Child's name)* sit the exam. We deeply regret this decision. She was not focussed and at her best and the examination result sadly demonstrates this fact. We just thought it was nerves, but on reflection we now realise that *(Child's name)* was under considerable emotional strain and very anxious about her aunt. If she had sat the 11+ examination under normal circumstances she would have passed.

(Child's name) sat a mock 11+ examination at *(name of school)* before the traumatic events unfolded. We were very concerned to see a significant drop in her maths score in the actual 11+ examination. She scored 117 in the mock exam and only 105 in the real examination. This fluctuation in performance is so significant as to leave us with no other conclusion. It was as a result of her emotional state at the time.

(Child's name) is a well-rounded individual who takes a keen interest at school and has attended the after school club for 5 years which runs various activities. She has attended *(style of)* dancing after school for *(time period)* and is in the school choir. She is supportive of her friends and her teachers have advised us that she always cares for the younger one's in the playground.

We believe *(Child's name)* deserves a place at a grammar school, as it is circumstances that have conspired against her to deny her the opportunity. Given her academic ability a grammar school education will best help *(Child's name)* to fulfil her potential.

Example 12 - Circumstantial

Appeal for *(Child's name)* **(Date of birth dd/mm/yy)**

I wish to appeal against the decision not to offer my son *(Child's name)* a grammar school place on the grounds that he did not achieve the required score of 111. *(Child's name)* was given an average standardised score of 106. (Non-verbal Reasoning 100, Verbal Reasoning 105, Mathematics 112).

All the indicators suggested that *(Child's name)* should have passed the 11+. His school reports show that he continues to work beyond the targets for his age and should attain level 5 in all three core subjects at Key Stage 2 SATS, demonstrating a particular ability in mathematics.

As well as being above average academically, *(Child's name)* is an excellent all-rounder. He adores sport and is captain of *(name)* FC's Under 11s team as well as playing for *(name)*'s football team. *(Child's name)* has also represented the school in athletics and swimming - last month he achieved the highest award (gold) in the *(name of competition)*. In the arts, *(Child's name)* is gaining confidence on the violin through private lessons held at school and was chosen to play and sing with the school choir this Christmas. He is also a keen participant in school drama productions. *(Child's name)* is a popular boy with an easy-going personality and caring nature who has been a credit to his school.

During his short period of preparation for the 11 + *(Child's name)* impressed us with his quick development of verbal and non-verbal reasoning skills. By mid September, *(Child's name)* was consistently achieving 85% or above in all NFER practice papers. His level of accuracy, speed and skill had developed well. We were expecting his results to continue to improve, but the month leading up to the exams became so stressful that *(Child's name)*'s performance suffered drastically and started to deteriorate.

It all began with an accusation that was levelled at *(Child's name)* in school about some graffiti found in the boys' toilets. The unfortunate outcome was a two-day exclusion (letter enclosed). This was both humiliating and destructive for *(Child's name)* as he tried to prepare for the examination. He was very upset, distressed and unable to focus on his preparation. At home, he frequently cried over what was happening at school. He had been repeatedly subjected to intense interrogation by senior staff and had to suffer the taunts of other children, who were aware that *(Child's name)* had been singled out in connection with the accusations. This affected *(Child's name)*'s friendships on a daily basis and was very demoralising for him. He was finally forced to suffer the indignity of an exclusion from school.

We believe this event severely affected the outcome of the examination and ruined his chance of succeeding. For *(Child's name)* it was a major life event, as it was the worst punishment the school could inflict and the stain on his school record can never be removed. This was even more difficult for *(Child's name)* to accept because he

50

has maintained throughout that he was not responsible for the graffiti. Those who are experienced at investigating more serious misdemeanours would have dropped the accusation immediately as there was no substantial proof he was ever involved.

Even though it was an unproven accusation based upon hearsay and dubious circumstantial evidence with no eye-witnesses, the school decided he was guilty and carried out the punishment without considering the consequences. It has now turned into a major dispute involving the governors, local authority and the school itself, which is still ongoing (see enclosed letter). We are determined to seek justice and redress after what has been done to our child. Poor *(Child's name)* was subjected to all this in the middle of trying to prepare for an important examination. It is no wonder he failed.

The exclusion came as a complete shock and *(Child's name)* was mortified. Prior to this, there had never been any suggestion that he had written graffiti, nor had he ever been accused of any bad behaviour. In fact quite the opposite as *(Child's name)* has regularly received merits for outstanding achievement and behaviour (some certificates enclosed). *(Child's name)*'s behaviour has always been exemplary at school.

Following these disastrous events *(Child's name)*'s confidence and motivation was in tatters. He was very depressed and found it impossible to lift himself into a frame of mind that would enable him to achieve anything resembling his best. We believe *(Child's name)* is deserving of a grammar school placement, as he would have achieved an outright pass, if the circumstances had been favourable.

Example 13 - Circumstantial

Appeal for *(Child's name)* (Date of birth dd/mm/yy)

We wish to appeal against the decision not to offer *(Child's name)* a place at any of the *(name of borough)* schools on the grounds that he did not attain the required score of 111.

(Child's name) is a talented, intelligent and industrious child. However, he has faced some setbacks that have disrupted his development. He has needed to make significant adjustments to life in England after the family migrated from *(country)* in *(year)*. This was further complicated by the emotional turmoil he suffered because of a life threatening illness I suffered over the ensuing two-year period (see enclosed letter from doctor). This crisis definitely affected his progress at school and his class teacher noted this at the time (see enclosed letter from head teacher). He feared he might lose his father and expressed this to his mother on a number of occasions. We believe these circumstances affected his educational progress significantly and it has taken him some time to recover. Despite this he has done well in his career at school and, more recently, has progressed at a remarkable rate.

Despite the difficulties *(Child's name)* has experienced, the head teacher and class teacher of *(name of child's school)* have no hesitation in supporting our appeal. His recent improvement has meant that *(Child's name)*'s school can confirm that they expect *(Child's name)* will attain level 5s in all the three core subjects in the forthcoming SATs tests. The school has also confirmed that he is already performing at level 5 in Mathematics and at upper level 4s in English and Science, whilst we are still more than five months away from SATs tests. (See enclosed letter from head teacher).

We purchased NFER practice papers and *(Child's name)* seemed to do well on these, achieving over 85% in mathematics, verbal reasoning and non-verbal reasoning. As parents, we do note however, a tendency for *(Child's name)* to be inconsistent at times. Again, we put this tendency to be unfocussed and listless down to his traumatic early life experiences. We hoped this inconsistency would not surface in the examination but it evidently did.

(Child's name) is very keen on extra curricular activities and we have encouraged this as much as possible. We believe it will mitigate his earlier experiences and help him to become a more rounded person. He reads music and plays violin well. He also plays badminton at *(name of sports club)* and is likely to be chosen to play for *(name of county)* next year. He is also very keen and enthusiastic in other sports viz. football, swimming, karate and ten-pin bowling. His artwork was selected for sale at the school fund raising event.

We look forward to hearing from you on the progress of our appeal.

Example 14 - Circumstantial

Appeal for *(Child's name)* (Date of birth dd/mm/yy)

We wish to appeal against the decision not to offer our son *(Child's name)* a place at *(name of school)* on the grounds that he did not reach the 111 threshold for entry (*(Child's name)* scored 106).

(Child's name) is an able, well motivated and highly conscientious child. He has made exceptional progress in his current primary school and we believe he will achieve Level 5s in the three core subjects of Mathematics, English and Science in his SATs in May of *(year)*. *(Child's name)* should have passed the 11+ examination. We believe there are very specific reasons why he did not achieve the required score.

(Child's name) is a very sensitive child and the trauma our family has undergone over the last year has severely affected his performance. It is unusual for a child to be given an award for kindness (see certificate) but this is well deserved for *(Child's name)* constantly puts the concerns of others before his own. This leads him to worry and become stressed if those around him are experiencing difficulties. This is even more pertinent if it involves our family.

Over the last year there have been times when *(Child's name)* has under achieved. *(Child's name)* as an only child desperately wanted a younger brother or sister like other children in his school. In *(month and year)* we found out *(Child's name)*'s mother was pregnant. This was a very joyful moment for *(Child's name)*. However it was tinged with sadness because shortly after we were told there was a high risk the baby may have *(name of medical condition)*. We faced the choice of deciding to have the baby or terminating the pregnancy at a late stage.

(Child's name) was just as distressed about this as we were. During our pregnancy we were constantly in and out of hospitals and after lot of tests and consultations it was decided the baby was a low risk to *(name of medical condition)*. Our baby was born on *(date)* (prematurely), but was then rushed to hospital on *(date)* with breathing problems and diagnosed with baby broncalitis. *(Child's name)* visited the baby and was very distraught at this point, particularly when he saw his baby brother with tubes attached to him and knew he might die. For weeks up to the point *(Child's name)* was not happy at school and even complained about going to school. Before all happened *(Child's name)* was a happy and contented little boy with lots of confidence. This whole experience has been very damaging for *(Child's name)* and has affected his performance at a most crucial point in his development. The whole period of disruption lasted for the whole length of the pregnancy and into the first weeks after birth.

We have recently moved home and *(Child's name)* started a new school in *(month and year)*. He has gradually got back to normal and has settled in well but the 11+ examination was a stressful time for him. Not only did he have to cope with the prospect of the loss of his baby brother, but also the loss of his school friends. He has needed to regain his confidence and make new friends too. He is gradually getting back to normal, but this takes time and the 11+ examination came at this wrong time for him.

We believe *(Child's name)* is an intelligent child who should be given the opportunity of a grammar school education and under normal circumstances would have passed this examination.

Example 15 - Circumstantial

Appeal for *(Child's name)* (Date of birth dd/mm/yy)

We wish to appeal against the decision not to offer our daughter *(Child's name)* a place at a *(name of school)* on the grounds that she did not attain the required pass score of 117 (score of 87).

We believe *(Child's name)*'s catastrophic failure in the 11+ examination is directly linked to our marital difficulties over the past few months. Her total inability to engage with the examination was completely out of character for *(Child's name)*. She was withdrawn, tearful and deeply troubled throughout this period. It is obvious the full impact of what was happening was directly expressed in her lack of ability to focus or concentrate in the examination.

The pressure of rows, ill feeling and tension in the home between my wife and I had also spilled over into angry scenes with *(Child's name)*. Tantrums were frequent and *(Child's name)* would also refuse to talk or discuss anything, preferring solitude. We were extremely worried about her, as we knew that she could not understand or psychologically process what was happening.

The poor relationship in our marriage almost led to physical separation and *(Child's name)* was obviously worried about the custody battle that was likely to ensue. Our two families were also involved and a great deal of resentment had built up between all the parties concerned. *(Child's name)* is very close to my parents and she was very worried she may not see them for long periods.

Her head teacher expressed concerns earlier in the year about the family situation and the possibility of involving the social services was mooted. However, after consultation with both my wife and I, *(Child's name)*'s head teacher decided not to call in social services, but informed *(name of town)* Health Services who arranged for close monitoring of the situation (see enclosed documentation). They have continued to take an interest in case any more concerns are raised.

All this was happening whilst *(Child's name)* was preparing to sit the 11+ examination. The effect of the problems at home was obviously devastating for *(Child's name)*. It is no wonder it all went wrong, although it is easier to understand it in hindsight. We should have postponed the examination until things were more stable for her and she was well enough to take the examination, but my wife and I were finding it very difficult to think clearly at the time for obvious reasons.

Despite the difficulties *(Child's name)* has experienced, she has shown herself to be a high calibre student. She is academically well above average and has continually strived to succeed at school. Her attitude and performance have been exemplary and the school has predicted that she should attain a level 5 in all three core subjects in her SATs in May. In the school environment *(Child's name)* radiates confidence and maturity as seen in various plays presented at her school where she has been cast as a main character. Music is also one of her passions and this Christmas she gave a solo piano recital at the school pantomime. We believe *(Child's name)*'s academic ability and talents would best be developed in a grammar school environment.

Although things have improved between us there still resides a fear in *(Child's name)* that this may happen again especially as relations between the families are still tense. Since the exams she has virtually closed off from all discussions relating to her future and finds solitude in her school activities. One unifying factor in our reconciliation has been our focus on *(Child's name)*'s academic progress. *(Child's name)* has seen unity and closeness growing between all of us over the last few months. However, we believe *(Child's name)* still harbours a fear that a future in our relationship would destroy that which she holds most dear; our family. Due to this inherent fear we believe *(Child's name)* still needs time to heal, as she remains more withdrawn than usual.

In the light of the circumstances under which *(Child's name)* sat the 11+ examination, we request a re-sit for her sometime next year. Due the trauma *(Child's name)* has undergone, we believe she still needs time to recover and suggest Easter next year as a suitable time to aim for. We understand this is an unusual request to make in an appeal, but we believe it is only fair that *(Child's name)* should be given an opportunity to demonstrate she has the ability to pass the grammar school examination under normal circumstances.

Example 16 - Circumstantial

Appeal for *(Child's name)* **(Date of birth dd/mm/yy)**

I wish to appeal against the decision not to offer *(Child's name)* a place at Grammar school on the basis that did not achieve the required score of 121 (scored 116).

(Child's name) is a hard working, conscientious and academically capable girl. She is a committed and self motivated individual who will always try her very best in all she does. We are hopeful that *(Child's name)* to do well in her SATs tests this May even though she has had to cope with the breakdown of our marriage towards the end of last year.

Despite these difficulties, *(Child's name)* has more recently been working at high-level 4/5's in all the three core subjects of English, maths and science. Fortunately for *(Child's name)* the difficult home circumstances she was experiencing last year have now eased. It is an known educational fact that children improve about two thirds of a SATs level each year, so we are now expecting *(Child's name)* to achieve three straight level 5's in her SATs. We were of course very disappointed when *(Child's name)* did not succeed in the 11+ in November, but it was hardly surprising considering the circumstances she was facing at the time of the examination.

During *(year)*, my parents helped us purchase our first home and we settled happily into a stable family life. *(Child's name)* was happy, quickly made new friends with local children and neighbours and enjoyed regular visits from other close family members. Unfortunately by the beginning of this year, my relationship with my husband had deteriorated significantly. We tried desperately to keep things on track for the sake of the children, but by June of this year things were so tense, we temporarily separated.

Unfortunately, a series of misunderstandings that led to a bitter dispute with my own family, forced me to move out of our family home too. In *(month)* of this year, we were forced to move into a much smaller property, which *(Child's name)* disliked intensely as we had to leave many of her things behind. She also lost all her friends and the wider family support she had enjoyed from grandparents, aunts and uncles. Initially my husband joined us, but the daily round of arguments, led him to finally move at the end of the summer and now divorce proceedings are pending.

The impact of these events on *(Child's name)* was devastating. It was very difficult enough for *(Child's name)* to cope with the break up the family, but she also had to deal with the loss of her father and the family home too. She was distraught and very tearful at the time. I tried to explain things to her, but she could see no logic in the decisions. Although *(Child's name)* had been seriously disturbed by the arguments and rows at home, she desperately missed her father when he finally left. *(Child's name)* became listless and began to withdraw for long periods. She also expressed her feelings and frustrations in frequent fits of anger and rage.

(Child's name)'s life was turned upside down this year and it is no wonder that her

performance at school and in the 11+ examination was seriously affected. *(Child's name)* was under enormous emotional strain at the time and deeply disturbed by events at home. It is a testimony to her that she did as well as she did in the exam. She was unable to prepare herself mentally for the examination and could not even bring herself to do standard practice papers from W.H Smith at home.

When we received the results *(Child's name)*'s teacher urged us to appeal for a place at *(name of school)*, as she thought *(Child's name)* was able to pass to examination. I did not submit the forms initially as I considered moving far away, so we could all make a fresh start. However, as no suitable employment could be found I have decided we will stay in *(name of county)*.

We strongly believe that under normal circumstances *(Child's name)* would have passed the 11+ examination comfortably and is fully deserving of a grammar school place.

Example 17 - Circumstantial

Appeal for *(Child's name)* **(Date of birth dd/mm/yy)**

I wish to appeal against the decision not to offer *(Child's name)* a grammar school place on the grounds that she did not achieve the required score of 121 *(Child's name)* scored 120).

(Child's name) is a very bright, highly motivated and academically able child. She has performed very well throughout her primary schooling and consistently achieves high grades in all subject areas. She is expected to achieve level 5 in all three core subjects in her SATs tests in May of *(year)*. I have included a report from *(Child's name)*'s head teacher to substantiate her academic ability. She is fully supportive of my appeal and believes *(Child's name)* should have easily passed the 11+ examination. It was a great disappointment for *(Child's name)* to find out that she missed the pass score by just one mark.

I believe there are mitigating circumstances that have a direct bearing on *(Child's name)*'s performance in this examination.

My wife and I have recently separated and this has been extremely painful for *(Child's name)*. She had always enjoyed a particularly close relationship with her mother. My wife had been spending most of her time away from the family home. She has since moved out and is now living with someone else. Divorce proceedings are now pending. *(Child's name)* was enthusiastic about visiting prospective grammar schools and found it very difficult when her mother, uncharacteristically, declined to be involved in the process. She was terribly disheartened and did not feel supported. She really wanted to succeed in the exam, but was not her usual happy self during this period. The domestic problems were continually affecting her motivation and state of mind.

During the run-up to exams, *(Child's name)* was in emotional turmoil. She had no idea where she would end up living or what primary school she might be sent to. Although her mother had packed up most of her possessions, the issue of custody had not yet been finalised. There had also been a number of disturbing and traumatic events in the home. *(Child's name)* witnessed serious rows, flare ups and some aggressive incidents which left her very distressed. Her sleep patterns were erratic and she cried a great deal during the night. *(Child's name)*'s relationship with her mother had seriously broken down. Her world had collapsed and she was very insecure, fearful and emotionally unstable.

The difficulties *(Child's name)* was experiencing at home were picked up at school. The head teacher was so concerned about *(Child's name)*'s welfare that she organised special support and counselling and this is still ongoing.

I believe that *(Child's name)* was seriously affected by these traumatic events during the run-up and the examination period. *(Child's name)* is an able, intelligent child who would highly prize the opportunity of a grammar school education. I am convinced that had *(Child's name)* sat the 11+ examination under normal circumstances she would have passed with a very high score. *(Child's name)* is very competitive and loves being involved in everything in her current school. She is still very determined to succeed in everything she does despite these domestic setbacks.

Example 18 - Circumstantial

Appeal for *(Child's name)* (Date of birth dd/mm/yy)

We wish to appeal against the decision not to offer *(Child's name)* a grammar school place in a *(name of school)* on the basis that she did not achieve the required score of 111 (score of 105).

(Child's name) is a bright, articulate and well motivated child. She has a dedicated approach to her work and has done well in all subject areas at school. *(Child's name)* is currently working hard to achieve SATs level 5s in the three main core subjects in May of *(year)*.

During the run up to the exam in November *(year)*, *(Child's name)* achieved average scores of around 85% in Verbal and Non-verbal Reasoning NFER practice Test Papers. I was fairly confident *(Child's name)* could achieve a pass and was very disappointed when she missed it by a few marks. *(Child's name)* also sat practice tests at school and did very well in these. We were encouraged by *(Child's name)*'s school to sit for the grammar school exams and at the time they were confident she could do well too.

There are some family circumstances that may have some bearing on *(Child's name)*'s performance. On the *(date)* this year, *(Child's name)*'s uncle died suddenly of a heart attack (see enclosed documentation). *(Child's name)* was very close to her uncle and was very fond of him. He was like a second father to *(Child's name)* and paid weekly visits to support *(Child's name)* in her schoolwork. This was a huge loss to *(Child's name)* and occurred right at the moment she needed the most support. I am severely dyslexic and not very well either, so this meant there was no other real support for *(Child's name)* in the home at this crucial time.

(Child's name)'s home circumstances are quite difficult generally. She is an only child and although my health is poor, I have to spend a great deal of my time looking after my elderly mother who also lives in the house. Her relationship with her father is often strained and very tense because he drinks too much and can be verbally abusive towards *(Child's name)*. Due to the home environment, none of *(Child's name)*'s friends can come to the house, so she often feels quite lonely. Therefore the death of her favourite uncle was very emotionally distressing for *(Child's name)* and affected her motivation. She was definitely not herself during this period and all her other schoolwork began to suffer also. She had lost a major support network in her life.

I believe *(Child's name)* deserves a chance and if given it will thrive in a Grammar School. I am confident she would become an integral and constructive member of such a community. *(Child's name)* is very determined to succeed in all she does despite all the difficulties she faces at home. A grammar school would provide a stable and high achieving educational environment for *(Child's name)* and we believe this is the best option for her.

Special Circumstances

NFER Recommendations

Examples of Appeals

Special Educational Needs
(e.g. ADHD or Dyslexia etc.)

NFER Secondary Selection Tests

Guidelines on Arrangements for Pupils with Special Educational Needs and Disabilities

Some pupils who apply to enter a secondary selection procedure may be considered to be at a disadvantage due to the testing arrangements that would normally apply. NFER issues the following guidelines to schools and local education authorities (LEAs) concerning the issue of special arrangements for such pupils. However, the National Foundation for Educational Research cannot accept any liability arising from the use of the guidelines contained in this document howsoever arising. It remains the responsibility of the LEA or school conducting the selection to ensure that their selection procedure for Special Educational Needs are in accordance with the Code of Practice contained in the Disability Discrimination Act 2001. The use of these guidelines cannot be relied upon by the LEA or school as ensuring that their procedures are in accordance with the requirements of the Disability Discrimination Act.

The Special Educational Needs and Disability Act 2001 requires responsible bodies to take reasonable steps to ensure that disabled pupils are not placed at a substantial disadvantage. In deciding which pupils should be granted special arrangements, it is recommended that schools or LEAs should refer to the guidance within the Disability Discrimination Act Code of Practice (Schools). The provision of special arrangements should be based on the on-going support that individual pupils normally receive and therefore, wherever possible, the test conditions should mirror those in which the pupil normally works. Such decisions would typically be based on evidence gathered over a period of time by the pupil's school, although there may be a need to evaluate information provided from outside of the school that is presented closer to the time of testing. The responsible authority should ensure that such information is from an appropriate professional source.

Some examples of special arrangements are large-print tests for visually-impaired pupils, an amanuensis for pupils with a writing difficulty, and extra time for pupils with a statement of special educational needs that indicates this is necessary. Other arrangements may include rest breaks, the use of a reader, or a longer practice period. Generally, schools are advised to offer the same level of support as would be given in normal classroom practice. Special arrangements that offer candidates an unfair advantage over others or that give rise to misleading information should not be made. Where extra testing time is allowed, this should not normally exceed an extra 25 per cent.

Because it may not be able to be established for certain that the special arrangements perfectly compensate for the nature and extent of the disadvantage, the special testing arrangement should be noted alongside the test score, and taken into account in any borderline decision.

Consideration should always be given to the individual needs of pupils. In all the above, it is assumed that the school or LEA has taken the decision in the first place that the test papers and their method of administration constitute a suitable form of assessment for the disadvantaged pupil. In certain circumstances, it may be decided that a test is wholly inappropriate for a particular pupil.

Therefore, whilst the responsibility for the selection procedure rests with the school or education authority, NFER's recommendation is that all results must be interpreted in the light of the specific circumstances of individual pupils and a professional judgement made.

February 2003

Example 1 - Special Educational Needs

Appeal for *(Child's name)* (Date of birth dd/mm/yy)

We wish to appeal against the decision not to offer our son *(Child's name)* a place at *(name of school)* on the grounds that he did not achieve the required pass score of 111 (*(Child's name)* scored 106).

(Child's name) is an able, well motivated and highly conscientious child. He has made exceptional progress in his primary school and we believe he will achieve Level 5s in the three core subjects of Mathematics, English and Science in his SATs in May this year. *(Child's name)* should have passed the 11+ examination. We believe there are very specific reasons why he did not achieve the required score.

(Child's name) has dyslexia as confirmed by the Dyslexia Institute in *(year)*; details of which are given in the information provided and supporting letter they have written. He has received two hours extra support a week from this agency since he was seven years old. *(Child's name)* has also received some support from his school for this problem, via the Learning Support Assistant, with measured targets set by the SENCO.

(Child's name)'s difficulties centre on reading and processing complex information. The Dyslexia Institute have identified specific weaknesses in working memory, mental control and auditory perception. However, *(Child's name)* is able to solve maths problems very well (e.g. fractions, percentages, ratios), if these are presented to him in number format. If he is given enough time he can also decipher the written text and answer complex mathematics and verbal reasoning problems without difficulty. In fact the Dyslexic institute has confirmed that *(Child's name)* has strengths in verbal reasoning and knowledge, perceptual organisation and speed of processing information.

After the results came through we were naturally very disappointed, but then disturbed when we discovered, quite inadvertently that *(Child's name)* should have been given more time in the examination, to compensate for his disability. Another parent, whose child has dyslexia and attends the Dyslexic Institute, informed us that her child had been given an extra fifteen minutes on every paper and had passed. We were never informed by his school that this special requirement should have been made available to *(Child's name)* even though they were fully aware of his difficulties. We now believe our child has been seriously disadvantaged in this examination and if this is not taken into account, it will not be a 'fair' result.

In the run-up to the examination *(Child's name)* had completed NFER practice papers and was attaining scores ranging between 80-98% in Verbal Reasoning, Mathematics and Non-verbal Reasoning. However, for these scores to be achieved there was always a run over of about 10-15 minutes on each paper. There were always questions he had not completed and he also needed time to re-check his answers. We know for a fact that *(Child's name)* did not complete the papers in the actual 11+ examination. He left out about ten questions on each of the Mathematics and Verbal Reasoning papers. Nevertheless, he still managed to obtain the respectable scores of 106 in mathematics and 104 in Verbal Reasoning. *(Child's name)* left out even more questions on the Non-verbal Reasoning paper, and yet remarkably this is where his highest score of 107 was achieved.

(Child's name) has worked very hard in the last four years to overcome his difficulties. His initial assessment at 7 years 2 months at the Dyslexic Institute identified that he was up to three years behind educationally. This was confirmed by his school who already knew that *(Child's name)* was having serious problems accessing the curriculum. *(Child's name)* is a very determined child and will let nothing stop him. His progress has been nothing short of astounding and despite continual difficulty he now holds his own with the very brightest children in his class. In fact, *(Child's name)* has just been moved up a maths group as recognition of his achievements.

(Child's name) has never allowed his disability to hold him back. When he started school he thought he was 'stupid', as his peers were always ahead of him. Now he knows why things were so difficult and has proved to himself he is more able than many of them. He specifically asked to sit the 11+ examination, despite the level of stress and difficulty doing this kind of test causes him. *(Child's name)* knows he is very bright and given the right opportunities has the potential to be a high achiever.

We believe *(Child's name)* is fully deserving of a grammar school place. If he had been allocated the extra time he was entitled to, he would have easily scored the five extra marks required for a pass. We are sure that grammar schools do not wish to discriminate against 'disadvantaged' children with ability but give them every opportunity to succeed. *(Child's name)* is a very talented child who knows for certain he should be educated in a grammar school. We, as his parents, believe that what has happened to him is unfair and unacceptable.

We wish to attend the hearing of the panel to further clarify any points that may be relevant to this appeal.

Example 2 - Special Educational Needs

Appeal for *(Child's name)* (Date of birth dd/mm/yy)

We wish to appeal against the decision not to offer *(Child's name)* a grammar school place on the basis that he did not achieve the required score 111 (*(Child's name)* scored 106).

(Child's name) is a well motivated, very bright and academically capable boy. He has made very good progress throughout his primary school education. We are confident *(Child's name)* will achieve level 5s in all three core subjects of English, Mathematics and Science in his SATs this year. It was very disappointing to learn that *(Child's name)* had not attained the required score for entry to grammar school. We believe there are very specific circumstances that led to his failure to achieve a pass score.

It was confirmed on *(date)* that *(Child's name)* suffers from Attention Deficit Hyperactivity Disorder (ADHD). This diagnosis was made by a Chartered Educational Psychologist after extensive testing, provision of educational information and discussion with a consultant paediatrician. We had suspected for some time that there was something wrong and this is why we sought a professional opinion. *(Child's name)*'s disability means he finds it very difficult to concentrate for long periods and can he easily distracted from tasks. He requires frequent breaks. Going from one assignment to another can also be problematic as he needs time to make the transition and settle into the new task.

This diagnosis has a direct bearing on any school tests and assessments that *(Child's name)* has done in the past. The undiagnosed condition means that *(Child's name)* has never had his special needs recognised or been given special consideration in any test or examination. This suggests *(Child's name)* has been significantly 'disadvantaged' in these situations and the results cannot be trusted as entirely fair or reliable. This to some extent calls into question end of year tests in school that attempt to assess SAT's levels as these may not be entirely accurate. However, to his credit *(Child's name)* has shown by stealth and tenacity that he is already achieving level 5 in Mathematics in school. Taking into account the real difficulty *(Child's name)* faced, a score of 106 in the 11+ examination was also highly commendable.

Whilst preparing for the examination, *(Child's name)* completed NFER practice tests in Verbal Reasoning, Mathematics and Non-verbal Reasoning and scored over 85% in every test. However, he was only able to do this if he was given more time. It often took some minutes for him to settle down and until he really got involved in applying himself to the test, he could be easily distracted.

We are aware that children with special learning difficulties, not related to ability level (as this is being tested) are given extra time and special consideration in the 11+ examination. *(Child's name)* needed this extra time and also to he seated in a space away from other children (not the normal examination room context) for him to achieve a true score. As we did not receive the diagnosis until after the examination

66

it was not possible to inform the relevant parties so these arrangements could he made. We are convinced that *(Child's name)* should have passed the 11+ examination without difficulty and is fully deserving of a grammar school placement. This is not a 'fair' result and *(Child's name)* has been 'disadvantaged' as he would have certainly scored the five extra marks required to pass.

Example 3 - Special Educational Needs

Appeal for *(Child's name)* (Date of birth dd/mm/yy)

We wish to appeal against the decision not to offer our son *(Child's name)* a place at a grammar school on the grounds that he did not achieve the required pass mark of 111 (*(Child's name)* scored 107).

(Child's name) is a very bright and capable boy who copes well with the challenges of his condition (detailed below). Despite this he has made good progress throughout his primary school education. It was very disappointing to learn that *(Child's name)* had not attained the required score for entry to grammar school. We believe there are very specific reasons why *(Child's name)* did not attain a pass score.

As a necessary background to this appeal, it is necessary to briefly cite *(Child's name)*'s educational history. Since *(Child's name)* appeared to be having difficulties with certain tasks in early schooling we began to seek assistance from professionals. In year one *(Child's name)* was found to be red/green colour blind. Further to this in *(date)* he was diagnosed with suffering from Developmental Co-ordination Disorder with multi-sensory processing and modulation difficulties. The diagnosis was made by a Consultant Paediatrician and later confirmed by an Occupational Therapist (see enclosed).

As a result we sought an intensive block of private sensory integration for *(Child's name)* to help him learn strategies to deal with his difficulties. This has had a positive impact on *(Child's name)*. Reports to this effect were forwarded from both his occupational therapists (NHS and Private) and the SENCO along with his grammar school application (see enclosed). *(Child's name)*'s disability means he has difficulty concentrating and focusing on tasks and requires prompts to enable him to do so. His condition also means that he requires frequent movement breaks to assist him with regulating his vestibular system and his performance can vary from hour to hour.

Since his 11 + examination our concerns have also led us to take *(Child's name)* to be assessed independently by a chartered educational psychologist (report enclosed), because we felt that his score did not reflect his academic potential. The educational psychologist has been able to identify both areas of both strength and weakness and made recommendations that will support *(Child's name)* with his learning. He states that *(Child's name)* has very high academic potential and comfortably sits within the top 2% of the population, when tackling verbal problem-solving skills. The educational psychologist also feels that *(Child's name)*'s underlying academic potential was not reflected in his score, as indicated in his confidential report. This was due to *(Child's name)*'s complex learning style and the fact that those setting the examination did not properly take some of these concerns into consideration.

We are aware that children with special learning difficulties, which do not relate to ability level, can be and usually are given extra time and special consideration in public examinations (see enclosed NFER recommendations following the passing of the Disability Act). *(Child's name)* needed the extra time, the use of an assistant reader for all the questions, regular prompts to ensure he remained on task and enlarged question and answer sheets for easier reading. *(Child's name)* initially was only granted extra time, but further discussions with the school following a letter (see enclosed) allowed *(Child's name)* to ask for some of the questions to be read to him and some prompting to be given to ensure he remained on task. They also agreed that the answer sheets would be enlarged.

In this respect there was a major failing, which significantly marred the other efforts that had been made to ensure the test was 'fair' for *(Child's name)*. *(Child's name)* claimed the enlarged photocopies, which incidentally included the question booklet and the answer sheet, were of poor quality. *(Child's name)* said they were blurred, faded in places and parts of questions were missing. This made the sheets very difficult to work with, so it is hardly surprising *(Child's name)* found things even more difficult. They had obviously been carelessly photocopied and not properly checked for errors. *(Child's name)* behaved as many children would, and did his best under the circumstances and finding it hard to pluck up the courage to complain at the time. It was only afterwards, he expressed how he was extremely upset and annoyed about the way he had been treated. Had the proper procedures been followed, we believe a truer score would have been achieved and *(Child's name)* would have passed the 11+ examination.

As *(Child's name)* was only placed on his schools Special Needs Profile in *(month and year)*, we feel that as his special needs have never been fully recognised in the past and that no special considerations have ever been made in any tests or examinations. This suggests *(Child's name)* has been significantly "disadvantaged" in these situations and the results cannot be trusted as entirely fair or reliable. It even calls into question his end of year test results that attempted to assess his SATs levels, as these may not be entirely accurate either.

Despite these difficulties and the unfair assessments he has been subjected to, *(Child's name)* has worked extremely hard to overcome his difficulties and is very determined to achieve a level 5 in all his subjects. Taking into account the real difficulties *(Child's name)* faces on a daily basis, a score of 107 in the 11 + examination was highly commendable. *(Child's name)* never allows his disability to hold him back in any area. As well as being determined academically *(Child's name)* is also a keen sportsman, even though he faces considerably difficult motor challenges.

(Child's name) worked very hard to prepare himself for his 11+ examination and completed NFER practice papers in all three subject areas. During this period he always required extra time to check over his work and ensure he had read the questions correctly. It was necessary to read the questions to ensure he had engaged with the task properly. Most of all, when we enlarged papers for him we always carefully checked the photocopies were clear and presentable. For *(Child's name)* this was the most important of all the things that should have been done for him and yet it was found to be the area of most lack. Under the proper conditions *(Child's name)* always performed well and would have performed equally well in the 11+ examination had this last and most important factor been taken properly into account.

We believe that *(Child's name)* is fully deserving of a grammar school place. If he had received the support required he would have gained a higher score. We are sure that grammar schools do not wish to discriminate against "disadvantaged" children with high ability, but give them every opportunity to succeed. *(Child's name)* is a very talented child who knows for certain that he should be educated in a grammar school. We, as his parents, believe that what has happened to him is unfair and totally unacceptable.

We wish to attend the hearing for the panel to further clarify any points that may be relevant to this appeal.

Example 4 - Special Educational Needs

Appeal for *(Child's name)* (Date of birth dd/mm/yy)

We wish to appeal against the decision not to offer our son a place at *(name of school)*, because he did not achieve the required score (216 out of 221).

(Child's name) is a highly motivated, intelligent and academically capable child who is deserving of a grammar school placement. He has put in an immense amount of effort to achieve high standards and to overcome the difficulties he has experienced educationally. We believe *(Child's name)* would have passed the 11+ examination had the conditions been favourable for him.

(Child's name) suffers from a developmental coordination disorder known as Dyspraxia. This affects his motor skills, causes attention and concentration difficulties and makes it difficult for him to stay on task. *(Child's name)*'s condition has been assessed by the NHS and a Dyspraxia diagnosis was confirmed on *(date)* (see enclosed report).

This report details that *(Child's name)* has difficulties in the following areas:
- Motor planning and sequencing of motor skills
- Weak hand strength
- Poor in-hand manipulation
- Hyper-mobile joints of the hand
- Poor pelvic stability

The condition causes *(Child's name)* considerable discomfort. He continually needs to adjust his sitting position due to pelvic instability and grip problems means he has to put writing implements down frequently. The occupational therapist's report observes that his performance may deteriorate during extended hand written pieces. This can obviously affect exam performance as it disturbs the normal process of moving from question to question and can have implications on timing.

(Child's name) was previously assessed by an educational psychologist whilst we were living in *(name of place)* (see enclosed report). This led to the NHS referral when we moved to the United Kingdom later that year. The report also details *(Child's name)*'s developmental coordination disorder and in particular highlights how his educational performance is affected by the condition. It clearly indicates that poor visual motor control and grip strength lead to problems with accuracy if he is pressed for time. To ameliorate the effect of such problems extra time is necessary to complete tasks accurately. This will compensate for the difficulties *(Child's name)* has with the sequencing and organization which are a natural corollary of such development coordination disorders. Since we are still waiting for the NHS to confirm *(Child's name)*'s next appointment we have taken him to see a chiropractor who is helping to treat this condition. His diagnosis is in agreement with the other professionals in involved in this case (see enclosed letter).

It is obvious from the NHS assessment and the report of the educational psychologist that *(Child's name)* is of above average ability. However, he has been considerably disadvantaged educationally by this condition. Despite these difficulties, *(Child's name)* has still performed well in all areas of the curriculum throughout the years of his primary education. He is predicted to achieve level 5 in the three core subjects of Mathematics, English and Science in his Key stage 2 SATs in May this year. He also did well on NFER practice papers (achieving in excess of 90% in verbal reasoning and non-verbal reasoning) on the run-up to the 11+ examination. We noted however that he did need more than the allocated time to achieve these high scores. So far his school has given him no special consideration for SATs and we are aware that time constraints may again affect his performance in May this year.

When *(Child's name)* sat the (name of school) examination, he did not complete the non-verbal reasoning paper. Had *(Child's name)* been able to complete this paper, we believe he would have passed the examination, as he only missed it by five points.

(Child's name) knows from his own experience that if he increases speed, his accuracy will suffer. This is confirmed by the educational psychologist who says quite categorically that where speed is necessary, a third party should be willing "to accept a less accurate product" (see highlighted section of report). We can only conclude that due to time pressures, *(Child's name)* was significantly disadvantaged in this examination.

In hindsight, we now know we should have applied for special consideration, as time became an important factor in *(Child's name)*'s performance. As we have so far not received any such recommendation from his school, we hesitated in this matter. Obviously, when the results came through we were very disappointed and regretted our decision. When we questioned *(Child's name)*, he then told us that he had had difficulty completing the papers. This was also our first experience of *(Child's name)* sitting a public examination and the confirmation of the professionals about *(Child's name)*'s condition became all the more evident when the results came through.

According to the admission requirements for *(name of school)* as issued in *(month and year)*, "All candidates sat the same test papers in conditions as near identical as could be reasonably arranged". Under normal circumstances such 'conditions' would have been fair but 'conditions' for *(Child's name)* would have needed adjustment, particularly with respect to time allocation to make it possible for him to be on a 'level playing field' with other children.

Given that fact that *(Child's name)* is of above average ability and demonstrated this by almost passing the *(name of school)* examination, we believe consideration should be given to the difficulties he faces educationally. On these ground we think *(Child's name)* should be offered a place, as an extra time allocation would have guaranteed a pass in the examination.

If offered a place, *(Child's name)* will prove a valuable member of the *(name of school)* community. He is a confident well adjusted child who works well on his own and with others. He is well liked by and popular with both is peers and with teachers. He is always compliant, loves a challenge and wants to succeed in everything he does.

Example 5 - Special Educational Needs

Appeal for *(Child's name)* (Date of birth dd/mm/yy)

We wish to appeal against the decision not to offer *(Child's name)* a grammar school place on the basis that he did not achieve the required score of 121 (achieved 107).

(Child's name) is an enthusiastic, energetic, hard-working child. Over the last few years he has worked diligently to improve his levels in Maths, Science & English. *(Child's name)* takes his studies very seriously and is particularly tenacious and determined to reach his full potential in everything he does. Although the head teacher predicts *(Child's name)* will only achieve a level 4 in KS2 SATs he has already scored a level 4B in year 6 past practice papers [Teacher's summary sheet]. This is indicative of his determination to succeed in the face of an identified learning difficulty.

We believe there are clear reasons why *(Child's name)* was unable to achieve the required score in the 11+ exam. *(Child's name)* is severely dyslexic. Although, the educational psychologist's report assesses *(Child's name)*'s general intellectual ability is in the top 25% of his peers [see report] it also confirms *(Child's name)* is suffering from acute dyslexia [see report]. The report categorised *(Child's name)* as Letter E on the Dyslexia index, which means he is severely dyslexic (ranges A-F: F being the worst case) [see report].

We were hardly surprised that *(Child's name)* did not pass the 11+, even though he was doing relatively well on familiarisation papers at home. We have been concerned for a long time about *(Child's name)*'s progress in literacy skills in particular, and decided to take him independently to the Dyslexia institute to get a professional opinion of his condition. This diagnosis has a direct bearing on any school tests and assessments *(Child's name)* has done in the past. On these grounds we believe *(Child's name)* has been severely disadvantaged in the 11+, given the findings of this consultation. The educational psychologist recommends his learning difficulties should have been taken into account to arrive at a reliable and fair result in the 11+ exam.

His teachers at *(name of school)* have continually been made aware of our concerns with regard to *(Child's name)*'s literacy skills, since he joined the school in year four. Although *(Child's name)* is an extremely bright, articulate child, his tenacity and diligence have probably masked the fact he was having so many difficulties. We have requested from the outset that more a detailed assessment and approach was needed to give him the extra support in reading and writing that he really needed, but this has never materialised.

It was judged by the school that *(Child's name)* was not a Special Needs case (although he clearly is) and would not therefore be entitled to a scribe or reader for any test he took. We have been informed by the head teacher that she really does not feel this is appropriate for *(Child's name)*, even though he has been assessed as severely dyslexic. The educational psychologist has clearly recommended extra-time, a reader and scribe for all public examinations [see report].

Despite the disadvantages *(Child's name)* faces he continues to make great efforts to improve. He is very interested in IT and loves doing internet research on science and seeks out maths games and puzzles, which he thoroughly enjoys and has a flair for. This strength has been picked up in the psychologist's report [see report]. We therefore believe *(Child's name)* would fit in well and flourish in a grammar school that specialises in Science and Maths.

(Child's name) has never allowed his disability to hold him back and he employs his own strategies to overcome his weaknesses. We feel that he would have achieved the pass mark had he been allotted the right provision over the years and during the 11+ testing. During the testing process, his understanding of questions would have been hampered and this would have slowed him down [see report], therefore he was in definite need of a reader and an amanuensis and extra time. We must also conclude that if *(Child's name)* had received the educational support he deserved right from the start, he would be much further along educationally than he is right now. Both his long-term development has been undermined by the lack of recognition his condition has attracted and also his recent performance in examinations.

(Child's name) is well deserving of a grammar school place and shows the intellectual ability that would be welcomed by a school such as *(name of school)*. We are sure that grammar schools do not wish to discriminate against 'disadvantaged' children if they have required ability level and potential to be successful academically.

Late Transfer

Right to sit 12+/13+ entrance examination

Examples of Appeals

Rejection of application to sit 12+/13+ entrance examination

Right to sit 12+/13+ examination

Children that have not sat for the 11+ examination have the right to sit the 12+/13+ examination. Entry is, however, subject to the availability of places. Counties or schools will often take up references from the schools the children are currently attending to assess the suitability of a candidate.

Some counties (e.g. Buckinghamshire) operate the 'Late Transfer Scheme' that does allow a child to sit the 12+ or 13+ even if they have failed in a previous year to pass the examination. Children can only sit once in an academic year. Again, references will be taken up from the school the child is attending to assess their suitability for a grammar school education. Level 5 in SATs is usually required as proof the child should have initially passed the examination.

The following appeals are as a result of being refused the opportunity to sit the examination. Persistence often wins through on these appeals as the examination will decide the final outcome anyway.

Example 1 - Late Transfer

Appeal for *(Child's name)* (Date of birth dd/mm/yy)

We wish to appeal against the decision not to allow our son to sit the 12+ examination on the following grounds:

(Child's name) is academically very bright and has consistently achieved high scores in all tests both in his primary and secondary education. In his primary school *(Child's name)* was placed in the top set and gained level 5's in the three core subjects of Maths, Science and English. As a year 7 student at *(name of school)* he is currently in the top sets of all the core subjects and furthermore he is placed in the highest band of those sets. He has already achieved level 6a in Maths and level 5 in science. We do not as yet have written confirmation of his achievements in other subject areas, although we have been told informally that his performance should be of a similar calibre.

We have been made to understand from the school *(Child's name)* currently attends that they do not wish to lose him as he is one of the brightest students in the year group, if not the very brightest. However, we believe their desire to hold onto *(Child's name)* should not be a factor in *(Child's name)*'s future. In other words, the school has a vested interest in holding onto *(Child's name)* and this should be taken into account in any decision with regard to *(Child's name)* being allowed to sit for the 12+. *(Child's name)* has the ability to achieve a grammar school place and should therefore be given the opportunity to sit for the 12+ examination.

The examination alone should decide this matter. We are aware that appeals use up valuable time, energy and resources for all concerned and would prefer the simplicity of the examination to decide this matter. However if it must go to an appeal panel please be assured of our determination in this matter. We will not rest until our son receives 'fair' treatment and for us this means the chance to sit the examination. We are aware of a number of other children in very similar circumstances who have sat for the 12+ and we do not see why our son who is extremely bright should not be given the same opportunity.

We believe that if *(Child's name)* is given the opportunity to sit for the 12+ he will prove himself worthy and win a place at a grammar school. *(Child's name)* has the right as an academically bright child to sit for this examination. We intend to ensure that he is not denied this opportunity to demonstrate his ability.

Example 2 - Late Transfer

Appeal for *(Child's name)* (Date of birth dd/mm/yy)

(Child's name) is an intelligent, well motivated and academically able child who is deserving of a grammar school placement. He is functioning at Level 6 in mathematics and level 5 in both English and science. Although he achieved 118 in the standardised test, we believe that this score is not representative of *(Child's name)*'s overall performance. In early practice tests he always achieved over 95% on every verbal reasoning paper. It is unfortunate that he failed to reach the required score on the day but we believe the academic evidence that supports his bid for a grammar school place is compelling:

1. A letter from *(Child's name)*'s headteacher at *(name of school)* (his previous school), fully endorses his academic ability.

2. An independent educational assessment that verifies *(Child's name)*'s academic ability and suitability for a grammar school education.

3. A strong letter of support from *(Child's name)*'s current headteacher at *(name of school)*. This letter is very welcome as it finally contains the admission there has been a serious mistake by the school in not placing *(Child's name)* in the correct sets. Although *(Child's name)* was initially assessed by the school to have a reading quotient of 120 (well above average) and to be of higher than average attainment he was mistakenly placed in lower sets. To his credit *(Child's name)* has worked his way up to the top sets in every subject area, although he should have been placed in them right at the start. *(Child's name)* now achieves A's and B's in every subject area and his teachers have noted that he is very able and hard working. One caveat must be noted however regarding this letter, as it claims that *(Child's name)* is functioning at level 5 in maths. We believe this to be a typing or administrative mistake as his maths teacher has verified that *(Child's name)* is functioning at level 6 in this subject (see letter from the maths teacher).

The mistakes in initial assessments and setting by his school meant there were excessive delays before *(Child's name)* was able to sit for the grammar school test - he was not originally deemed suitable for testing. It was hard for *(Child's name)* to stay prepared through the many months of waiting. The sudden decision to test him gave him insufficient time for adequate preparation. Under such emotional and psychological pressure it is not surprising he did not perform as well on the day as he had done in previous NFER practice tests (these had been completed many months before).

(Child's name)'s sister will be taking up a place at *(name of school)* in September 2004 and we are very much hoping that both children can attend the same school. *(Child's name)* has a special interest in science and mathematics and we note that *(name of school)* has been awarded Specialist Science and Mathematics Status.

78

Example 3 - Late Transfer

Appeal for *(Child's name)* (Date of birth dd/mm/yy)

Thank you for your reply of *(date)* to our letter.

Firstly, we were not aware there was a deadline for application. This was not explained to us when we initially contacted *(name of county)* Local Authority about the Late Transfer Scheme by telephone. Our initial enquiries were made at the beginning of the year and we should have been notified about this by your administrative team.

Secondly, as we were not aware of any time constraints we took our time in making the decision to have our daughter tested, However, we believe she is very able and should not be denied the opportunity to sit for a grammar school place this year.

Thirdly, we are aware of other children who have recently sat for this test, whose parents also did not apply before this deadline. We obviously cannot divulge names as this would compromise these children. However, it is not acceptable or fair for other children to have been given the chance to sit the test and our child to be denied it.

Fourthly, we do not see the point of waiting for *(year)* entry when *(Child's name)* is ready to sit for this test now. It will be very difficult to sustain her interest level until that time. She has done all the practice tests and is ready to sit.

Fifthly, we are in catchment as we live on the *(name of county)* border. We have a right to have our daughter tested and do not believe there should be a delay.

Sixthly, she has only one test to sit. This is not as difficult to organise as the previous arrangement where three tests were sat on three different days.

We do not wish to get into a protracted dispute but will appeal against the decision if we have to. A simple decision to allow her to sit will avoid wasting time, money and energy. We look forward to a positive response.

Example 4 - Late Transfer

Appeal for *(Child's name)* (Date of birth dd/mm/yy)

(Child's name) is a focused, well motivated, enthusiastic and disciplined child who is currently working at level 5 in English. The report submitted by *(name of school)* gives no information on his levels in either Maths or Science. It does however give a lot of other subject information which maybe of interest, but is not crucial in assessing *(Child's name)*'s ability. Full information should have been supplied on SATs levels in English, Maths and Science as these are the core subjects.

An oblique handwritten comment was made on the first report to indicate that *(Child's name)* is not suitable for a grammar school (copy of reports enclosed). The teacher who made this comment is only responsible for Maths and had no right to make a sweeping and unqualified remark about *(Child's name)*'s suitability for a grammar school education. Even the second report (requested by myself as I considered the first inadequate) still contained no SATs levels. A glaring omission considering, there was a willingness to make unsubstantiated statements about a child's future education.

At the end of Key Stage 2, *(Child's name)* was achieving level 4 in all the core subjects. It is a recognizable educational fact that most children go up two thirds of a level each year. *(Child's name)* is now achieving level 5 in English, which proves this point. Although we have no comment in the reports supplied by *(name of school)* on this crucial issue of levels for Science and Maths, is it not highly likely that *(Child's name)* is operating at level 5 in Maths and Science too? I would say 'yes' in the absence of comment from his school. This is obvious and they should have stated it.

A casual reading shows these reports to be inadequate, lacking in detail, biased in their comment and certainly not a fair representation of *(Child's name)*'s ability level. It is hard to know why such an unprofessional approach has been taken by the school in providing proper educational information. I have showed the reports to one or two other teachers who I know and who currently work in schools and they were not impressed.

In the absence of correct and reliable information, it is clear that only the test should decide whether *(Child's name)* goes to a grammar school. If reports are to decide then there is no need for a test. However, I would wish the report to be accurate first. In this case they are wholly misleading. I can only comment, that if the test alone is sufficient for the 11+, then why is it not sufficient for the 12+, particularly when the school has produced such an unreliable assessment of *(Child's name)*'s achievements so far.

I believe that if *(Child's name)* is given the chance to sit the 12+ examination he will prove himself worthy of a Grammar School place and I trust he will not be denied this opportunity.

Taking your Appeal Further

Letters to the Ombudsman

Example 1 - Ombudsman

Appeal for *(Child's name)* (Date of birth dd/mm/yy)

We wish to complain about the appeal panel's handling of the above appeal, which resulted in our son *(Child's name)* not being offered a grammar school placement.

(Child's name) was diagnosed as suffering from ADHD (Attention Deficit Hyperactivity Disorder) by a Chartered Educational Psychologist and a consultant paediatrician (report attached). This disability means *(Child's name)* finds it difficult to concentrate for long periods without being distracted. He should have been given extra time on each paper and been allowed to sit the papers under specifically non-distracting conditions (e.g. in a quiet room without other children present). Only with these special considerations in place could a true score be achieved. As the diagnosis was made subsequent to *(Child's name)* sitting his 11+ examination, these arrangements could not be made. As a result *(Child's name)* only scored 106 instead of the required 111 marks in the examination. We believe the circumstances under which *(Child's name)* took the examination to have led directly to his failure to achieve a pass score.

(Child's name) is a bright, intelligent child who is predicted to achieve SATs level 5 in all three core subjects in May of this year. In NFER practice tests he always scored in excess of 85% in Mathematics, Verbal Reasoning and Non-verbal Reasoning, but as expected required extra time on each paper to achieve these marks. The basis for our appeal was that *(Child's name)* would have scored the extra five marks in the 11+ examination if he had been given the extra time which was his right. The appeal panel should have focussed on this issue and tried to gauge whether this would have been the case.

This issue was not addressed by the appeal panel. The matter was brushed aside with no proper consideration of both the professional and academic evidence. Information was discussed throughout the appeal that had little or no relevance to the central issue that should have taken up the appeal panel's time. We came away from the appeal both frustrated and dismayed about the handling of our case.

We do not consider our appeal was fairly heard or properly considered. As a result, we believe *(Child's name)* has been subject to unfair discrimination on the basis of his special needs. If *(Child's name)* is bright enough to achieve the score for a grammar school placement, but has been disadvantaged by the format of the examination, this should have been recognised and given proper consideration by the appeal panel.

Example 2 - Ombudsman

Appeal for *(Child's name)* (Date of birth dd/mm/yy)

We wish to raise a complaint about the way the appeals procedure for our daughter *(Child's name)* was handled. Our appeal was not fairly heard or considered.

The key facts of our appeal were completely ignored during the appeal hearing. The leader of the appeal panel did not steer the committee correctly or curtail irrelevant discussion. As a result, all the most important facts of the appeal were overlooked in favour of trivial and less vital information.

We expected the committee to focus on the academic basis of our appeal as we had submitted strong academic evidence for consideration. Our appeal statement concentrated on the fact that *(Child's name)* is a high achiever who consistently maintains high grades. She only missed the required score of 111 by one mark (110). *(Child's name)* has the reading age of a thirteen year old and is already achieving level 5c in English. Maths and Science. *(Child's name)* has represented the school in a writing competition and was about to represent her school again in the *(Child's name)* Borough Maths Challenge. She is an excellent communicator and has highly developed, mental maths and problem solving skills. *(Child's name)* is undoubtably one of the most gifted and talented children in her school (a fact her school can verify). None of these matters was discussed or considered; and this was the basis of the appeal.

Instead, the committee spent a great deal of time discussing less relevant matters; *(Child's name)*'s interest in *(subject)* and *(subject)*, some medical matters and the fact that her older brother had gone to a Catholic comprehensive school took up much of the time. The committee even chose to dwell on my fund raising activities for *(name of school)*, which was totally irrelevant to the appeal. When we left the hearing we felt dismayed and disillusioned. It had run over time (40 minutes), and yet we felt throughout, that the committee was unfocussed and had not really discussed the main points of the appeal. We kept wondering when they would get to point and believed the extra time spent was genuine interest. However, when the appeal suddenly ended, we realised that there had never been an intention to discuss the relevant matters of our appeal.

We felt the process was unfair and and the decision unjust. We strongly believe that *(Child's name)* is deserving of a grammar school place. If the appeal had been heard fairly it would make it easier to accept the decision of the panel. As it is, we have no respect for the conclusions of the panel. The hearing should have followed the correct procedure and concentrated on the basis of the appeal. We wish this matter to be fully investigated, as we believe it is a serious breach of the rules governing appeals. We are willing to take the matter even further if our case is not properly considered.

Example 3 - Ombudsman

Appeal for *(Child's name)* **(Date of birth dd/mm/yy)**

We wish to complain about the appeal panel's handling of the above appeal, which resulted in our son *(Child's name)* not being offered a grammar school placement.

The basis of our appeal was as follows:

(Child's name) had attained a score of 118 instead of the required score of 121. We submitted strong academic evidence to support our appeal. Three letters were supplied; two from his headteachers and one independent assessment to show that *(Child's name)* is of grammar school standard. It was also clear from this material that *(Child's name)* is functioning at level 6 in maths and science and level 5 in English.

We believe *(Child's name)* was unable to fully demonstrate his academic potential for a number of reasons. Circumstantial evidence was provided showing the immense disruption *(Child's name)* had experienced in his schooling. *(Child's name)* had to adjust first to a new independent school and then state schooling after a move from *(name of country)*. He was then subjected to continual misunderstandings and mistakes by those responsible for his education in this country. This was further compounded by delays in the decision to test him for a grammar school place. *(Child's name)* had completed practice tests at least six months before he was allowed to sit the test. Given the unnecessary delays, it was very difficult to focus psychologically, emotionally and most important of all, academically for such a one-off, and for him momentous test.

Our appeal was not sympathetically heard and properly considered for the following reasons:

The LEA representative who was responsible for leading the appeal hearing displayed a negative and patronising attitude from the very beginning. He claimed that even though he had a summary prepared of the relevant documentation beforehand, it was confusing and hard to follow. The summary we have provided in the above paragraphs is simple enough. Indeed we had provided an up to date statement on which we considered the appeal should be based. This was not difficult or confusing to follow. It was misleading to the other members of the panel to make such an admission at the beginning of the appeal. It was clear that he had no real idea what the appeal should really concentrate or focus upon. We knew from this moment that we would not receive a fair hearing.

Throughout the presentation of evidence the LEA representative was constantly making disapproving gestures (sighing, shaking his head and pulling facial expressions). It was totally inappropriate for him to be commenting on the appeal in this way while it was in progress. It was as if the decision had already been made. This was particularly distressing as he was responsible for giving information about the selection process and other matters concerning the appeals process to less informed members of the panel. As leader of the panel he should have been acting in an impartial and even handed way throughout the hearing.

As was to be expected the LEA representative dismissed and disregarded the evidence that was submitted. The letters from the two headteachers and the independent assessor were discredited as being 'just written statements and subjective judgements'. It was totally unacceptable for him to treat the opinions of professional and qualified people in this way. The contents of these letters should have been considered seriously and been given full consideration. The prejudicial way in which this material was treated meant the contents were just brushed aside as irrelevant and unimportant.

When it came to summarising the appeal the LEA representative was unable to do it in succinct way. He spent about five minutes flicking through papers, but could not seem to find what he was looking for. He then made a brief comment in a joking manner that there was nothing to summarise. This is a clear indication that the appeal panel had not really considered the issues as no clear summary could be made of what matters the hearing had discussed.

Summary
We consider the appeal to have been 'unfair' and biased due to the inappropriate leadership and conduct of the LEA representative throughout the hearing. As a result the hearing failed to consider crucial evidence and focus on the essential elements of the appeal. We believe our son to be seriously 'disadvantaged' by the decision not to offer him a grammar school place. What is more; it is totally unacceptable to find this decision was made on the grounds of misinformation and prejudice, without due consideration of the facts.

Example 4 - Ombudsman

Appeal for *(Child's name)* (Date of birth dd/mm/yy)

I am writing about our recent appeal against the decision not to offer *(Child's name)* a place in the *(borough)* Grammar Schools. We felt the facts of the case were ignored and not listened to. Also, we felt the case was not understood at the time, nor sympathetically considered afterwards, which might have something to do with the fact that not all the panel appeared fully conversant with the technicalities or the practical running of the exam. In addition, the procedure was not followed as outlined in the 'Guidance for Parents'.

Refering to the enclosed 'Guidance for Parents' (1) the chairman did not outline the procedure to be followed, (2) the schools' representative did not provide a statement as to why *(Child's name)* had not been offered a place (3) and the lay member of the panel directed the proceedings for the majority of the time. This resulted in some confusion on our part as the procedure did not follow the format we had expected. Also we remain puzzled as to why it was essential that the order of preferences for the *(borough)* Schools be written on the appeal form. We felt such information prior to the appeal was irrelevant and could potentially bias a panel's decision. We should also point out that the multiple choice answer sheets are shredded after the exam so the panel could not verify that *(Child's name)* had made an error on the non-verbal reasoning paper.

The appeal was very brief. We were asked if *(Child's name)*'s school taught for the 11 plus, when we had thought of entering him for it and which subjects he enjoyed most. We were also asked about his scores on practice tests and if these tests were timed, whether we had tried to phone the school on the morning of the exam and if the journey to and from the *(borough)* schools would be a problem. It became apparent that the reason for our initial appeal was not going to be discussed. We had the distinct impression that a decision had been made about our case prior the appeal with a consequent lack of enquiry about the extenuating circumstances.

Our appeal was on circumstantial grounds in that *(Child's name)* had no sleep the night before the exam for reasons beyond our control. A letter from our G.P. and a statement by the schools' representative at the end of the appeal both confirmed that fatigue is definitely known to reduce performance. It would appear that such a statement made by two professionals was either ignored or disbelieved. The latter would be odd in view of the fact that we submitted a letter from Southern Electric verifying events. We know of two other successful cases which were similar to ours and this causes us to question the consistency of the panel's decision making process.

On a technical point (obviously not understood) we needed to explain to one member of the panel the implications of missing out a multiple choice question and then continuing to answer the next seventeen questions in the wrong boxes. On a practical point (obviously not understood either), the panel asked the schools'

representative what the normal procedure was if a child was sick during the exam and the representative acknowledged he was "learning all the time." The reply that should have been given was that the child could speak to a member of staff, go home and return another day. The fact that a medical certificate was mandatory in order to sit the exam later was not mentioned and we are not sure if the panel understood this fact. We added to the reply that, as parents, it was impossible to speak to staff as we were not allowed into the school building and the school was only contactable via an answerphone. This surprised the schools' representative who said arrangements at her school were different.

At the end of the appeal, the schools' representative made a point but we could not hear it fully. She was saying something about non-verbal reasoning testing abstract thought and *(Child's name)*'s favourite subjects. We were sitting nearest to her and no one on the panel followed it up. It would be of interest to know if the panel heard and understood this point and what was minuted.

In conclusion we feel the main issue of this appeal was not listened to and ignored for whatever reason. The procedure as set out in the 'Guidance for Parents' was not followed and some of the panel did not appear to understand a practical or technical point. We feel this resulted in an unfair decision and therefore question whether the process was fair. The grounds for *(Child's name)*'s appeal are genuine and verifiable. We were amazed that such a clear and justifiable case was not dealt with sympathetically.

Example 5 - Ombudsman

Letter to the Ombudsman

We believe our appeal was not fairly heard by the appeal committee. The appeal was circumstantial and the issues surrounding this were not sufficiently examined, due to misinformation conveyed to the other members of the appeal committee by the LEA representative. Due to this, the appeal centred around *(Child's name)*'s academic ability, which has never been in question. The real substance of the appeal, which was a family tragedy from which *(Child's name)* is still finding it difficult to come to terms with, were never properly explored.

We believe *(Child's name)* failed to perform academically for very specific reasons. However, the committee were given the impression that her academic ability was questionable because the NFER scores she had achieved in practice papers at school were completely invalid. The LEA representative stated that there was a substantive difference between the verbal reasoning test papers originally published by NFER and the LEA test papers that had been set. He claimed that the LEA test papers were more difficult than the NFER test papers and that *(Child's name)*'s high scores in these practice papers were therefore to be disregarded. This claim was a very damaging to our appeal, as it meant that the evidence we had presented became irrelevant to the committee.

I have investigated further into this matter and an educational expert has assured me, that there is no substantive difference in standard between NFER practice papers and the papers set by the LEA. The expert I have consulted has access to real test papers and can vouch for the fact that the types of questions that are set and the standard of the questions are the same. After all, there would be little point in providing NFER practice papers to the general public through major retailers if they were not providing real practice for children. This would be both unfair and misleading.

I have also checked with the National Foundation for Educational Research (NFER) on this matter. They have confirmed that they devise the papers used by LEAs and these have been standardised and tested on a cohort of children. Their own literature on verbal reasoning claims, and I quote, 'The tests have high reliability and are relatively good predictors of subsequent academic attainment'. They also clearly stated to me that although the practice tests have not been subjected to the same trials or standardisation, they are structured similarly, contain the same number of questions and use the same types of questions as the real tests. NFER claim the purpose of the practice tests is to familiarise children with the tests and to provide useful test practice. It is therefore hard to believe that the practice tests would provide no indication of a child's likely performance in the test, even if they were not subjected to the same rigour, since they have come from the same source. Tests that have the same type of structure and question content would not vary in standard to this degree. Half the questions are technique based anyway and it is impossible to make these questions harder in the test. If a child is bright enough to grasp how to do coding and letter sequencing questions, they tend to get them right on every paper. We found this to be the case with *(Child's name)*, who performed consistently well on all verbal reasoning papers before the circumstances I have described in the appeal occurred.

Therefore, the high-test scores achieved by *(Child's name)* in NFER practice papers that she sat in school do have validity and should have been considered as evidence of her ability. The information given by the LEA representative was misleading and severely damaged our appeal. It is clear from the academic record that *(Child's name)* should have passed this exam. The committee should have been focused on why *(Child's name)* did not perform, as she should have done. It is clear from the written evidence we presented, which was virtually ignored, that *(Child's name)* had been subjected to a very traumatic and disruptive life event, which had impacted her ability to do well in the eleven plus examination. We have enclosed our original appeal statement for your information and consideration. We also trust that after careful consideration our case will now be dealt with fairly.

Example 6 - Ombudsman

Letter to the Ombudsman

We believe our recent appeal hearing *(date)* was unfairly heard for the following reasons:

Our son *(Child's name)* has special needs, but he is a bright and capable child. We believe a child with special needs should be able to secure a grammar school place, if it can be shown that they would have achieved the score if their disability (providing it is not related to academic ability) had not prevented them. *(Child's name)* scored 107, only 4 marks short of a pass, even though he needed to overcome considerable physical and psychological disabilities (see-enclosed materials and appeal statement).

The grounds of our complaint concern the conduct of the deputy head (school representative) both before, throughout the course of and after the hearing. Both her manner and her comments were extremely biased and we believe would have made it very hard for the appeal panel to reach a balanced viewpoint and decision.

On our arrival at the hearing venue, we were immediately approached by the deputy head (school representative). We thought she was just introducing herself, but to our surprise she said she would like to discuss some aspects of the statement we had written, before the hearing began. We picked up from her curt and formal manner that she strongly disagreed with our statement and this was later borne out in the hearing. We do not think it is acceptable to be approached by the school representative before the hearing to discuss aspects of the case. We found this to be disconcerting, unsettling and intimidating. This was never followed up by the deputy head (school representative), but her actions left us confused and concerned she would not present the case fairly from the outset, as she appeared to wish to challenge our statement before we even entered the room.

The nature of her objection was soon apparent in the hearing. Some enlarged photocopies used by *(Child's name)* were produced in the hearing by the deputy head (school representative), and we were asked to examine them to see if they were acceptable to us. We were not able to check them all for quality, as we were only shown a small sample and to be honest the only person capable of making a judgement about this was not present – *(Child's name)* himself. The fact is *(Child's name)* said they were not good enough for him and he complained about them as soon as he returned from the examination. No relevant comments could possibly have been made that would have helped the panel on this issue, unless *(Child's name)* was there to point out the problem. This was obviously a personal affront to the deputy head (school representative) as she claimed that she organised the preparation of these photocopies and had supposedly checked them for quality. At this point, reference should have been made to the professional evidence we had submitted about the fact that yellow overlays would have made a tremendous difference. This was a fact that was not known at the time of the examination, but should have been taken into account by the appeal committee. The comments of the expert (report enclosed) were completely ignored and disregarded by the deputy head (school representative) and the panel were led into thinking our son's complaints had no foundation. This was a biased, sensationalised use of material, which did not allow a full examination of the evidence. The conduct of the deputy head (school representative) was totally unacceptable. We believe it seriously damaged our case and would have swayed the panel's thinking. One panel member seemed fixated on the photocopy issue asking questions repeatedly about this, which seemed to bear this out.

We were also astonished to find the deputy head (school representative) both during the hearing and in her summation continually made negative comments about our child. She said that when *(Child's name)* was allowed outside for his break it took three members of staff, one hour to get him back inside as he kept running off .We expressed concern at this comment, as *(Child's name)* does not display this type of behaviour. Even if true, which we doubt, it was irrelevant to the appeal and should never have been raised. The deputy head (school representative) also stated that the staff support member who had supervised the test claimed, "He was the worse special needs child she had ever met". We were truly astonished and angered by this comment, which again had no relevance to the appeal. If it be known, *(Child's name)* has only ever been offered limited support at school (which we are constantly asking to be reviewed) and has never caused any difficulties that cannot be managed within the classroom. We have never had complaints about his behaviour and were very distressed by these comments. Such negative comments were extremely damaging to our appeal and had no place in this hearing.

We were also very surprised to find the deputy head (school representative) making general comments about special needs provision. She expressed her concerns about whether or not it would be safe to have *(Child's name)* in the science laboratory or doing similar activities that had an element of danger. She went on to say that special needs at their school usually involved children who did not have English as their first language. We were truly appalled by these statements; as I am sure you are aware there is very clear guidance as to what is a "special need" in relation to the Code of Practice (schools) contained in the Disability Discrimination Act 2001. The attitude and comments of the deputy head (school representative) were discriminatory and smacked of prejudice and we found them offensive.

Even while we were waiting outside for the panel to make their decision and for *(Child's name)*'s school books to be returned to us, the deputy head (school representative) also made more irrelevant comments about another child with Aspergers at their school. We felt this bordered on breaching confidentiality. It is not unreasonable to assume we may be aware of the identity of this child, as the community of children with disabilities is quite small and contact is regular through parental support groups.

The appeal should be an attempt to explore whether *(Child's name)* could have passed, were it not for his disabilities. There was no attempt to examine the evidence pertaining to *(Child's name)*'s academic ability and the difficulties he faces in demonstrating this. Instead, the negative, unprofessional and irrelevant comments continually made by the deputy head (school representative) dominated this appeal and made it extremely difficult for the panel to make a fair decision.

THE AUTHOR

Stephen C. Curran MA, BA(Hons), B(Mus), PGCE, Dip. RSA, Mcot, has many years of teaching experience both in the Secondary and Primary sector. In addition to writing, Stephen runs courses for children in Mathematics, English, Verbal Reasoning and Non-verbal Reasoning.

Published by:
ae® Accelerated Education Publications Ltd
P.O. Box 40, Twickenham TW1 1UZ

Repro and printing by:
Imperial Printers UK Limited
Twickenham TW2 6QL

Visit our websites at:
www.aepublications.co.uk
www.aetuition.co.uk

ISBN 978-1-904257-72-1

WORKBOOKS IN THE SERIES...

11+ MATHS & TESTS

Basic Number	Lines and Angles
Number Relationships	Time
Decimals	Symmetry
Fractions	Shapes
Money and Costs	Perimeter, Area
Measurement	& Volume
Averages	Geometry
Bases	Tables, Charts,
Percentages	Graphs & Diagrams
Ratio & Proportion	Algebra
Probability	

MULTIPLICATION TABLES

15-Day learning programme
This book comes complete with 48 flash cards.

VERBAL REASONING

Alphabet Reasoning
Word Patterns and Codes
Vocabulary with Spelling
Vocabulary with Meaning
Logical Reasoning
Mathematical Reasoning

CREATIVE WRITING

Generating story ideas	The elements of story
Literary and grammatical devices	Voicing stories
	Story structure
Story dialogue	Story endings
Character development	

NON-VERBAL REASONING

Elements	Codes
Movements	Analogies
Manipulations	Similarities
Patterns	Series
Layering	Matrices
Components	Revision
Odd One Out	

SPELLING & VOCABULARY

Foundation Level

Intermediate Level

Advanced Level

This series of books provides a complete and comprehensive course which builds a child's spelling and vocabulary expertise to boost 11+ Verbal Reasoning, comprehension and word power skills.

ISBN 978-1-904257-72-1

9 781904 257721

Educational books produced by AE Publications are available from all leading booksellers or by mail order directly from the publisher

Visit:

www.aepublications.co.uk

Benson's Discovery

By

Olayinka Oyebode

Illustrated by

Shazeb Khan